The Cat and St. Landry

by Mary Alice Fontenot and Vincent Riehl

A biography of Sheriff D. J. "Cat" Doucet of
St. Landry Parish, La. (1936-1940; 1952-1968)

Illustrated with photographs

Baton Rouge
CLAITOR'S PUBLISHING DIVISION

ISBN Number 087511-683-3

First Printing, October, 1972
Second Printing, February, 1973
Third Printing, May, 1984
Fourth Printing, February 2020

For
Ruth Robertson Fontenot

Introduction

Public figures who become legends in their own lifetime are rare — Babe Ruth, FDR, Marilyn Monroe, John Dillinger, Louis Armstróng, Dr. Albert Schweitzer, Martin Luther King. Other lesser humans must die before they enter the pantheon of those about whom fanciful stories are told, some true, some apocryphal, all tinged with the aura of a strong and charismatic personality.

Sheriffs do not ordinarily make good candidates for legends, living or dead, unless one counts pseudo - folk figures such as Wyatt Earp, largely a tv - created phony, or the Sheriff of Nottingham. But in Louisiana, there is a former lawman who for three decades exerted a powerful political influence and whose deeds and picturesque phraseology are the subject of many a political conversation in Acadiana.

When people in Southwest Louisiana talk about "the Cat," they have only one subject in mind: Daly Joseph Doucet, better known as "Cat" Doucet, colorful, controversial sheriff of St. Landry Parish for 20 years, deputy sheriff for 12. "When they made Cat, they threw away the mold" admiringly say the ex-sheriff's supporters. His detractors say the same thing, and add "— thank God!"

Cat was personally picked by New Orleans Mayor deLesseps S. Morrison to be on the welcoming committee for General Charles de Gaulle when the French president visited New Orleans in 1960. Cat wound up on the cover of Life magazine, shaking hands with his countryman.

Cat was not always in such high cotton. Many, many years before that memorable day, he used to drive a cab in Opelousas, with a good portion of his business being salesmen (they called them "drummers" then) going and coming from the many houses of prostitution there. He also tried barbering and the railroad but it was only when he fell in with the Long boys - Huey and Earl — who gave him a job as game warden, that Cat hit his political stride.

The story of Cat Doucet and how he ran St. Landry Parish as his personal fiefdom for 20 years is fascinatingly told in a new book by Mary Alice Fontenot, long-time writer and newspaperwoman. In private life Mrs. Vincent Riehl (her husband aided

i

in the research and is co-author), she is the author of the charming and highly successful series of children's books about Clovis Crawfish and his bayouland friends. She utilizes the same detailed, even-paced style, laced with an easy sense of humor in "The Cat and St. Landry." The result is an absorbing tale of a man with humble beginnings, who achieves, then lustily wields the power he always craved for, surviving in the process the slings and arrows of political misfortunes, including a grand jury indictment of 32 counts.

Through the pages of "the Cat and St. Landry" roam the figures of many a well-known Louisiana politician — Huey and Earl Long, O.K. Allen, Jim Garrison, Bill Dodd, Chep Morrison, Sam Jones, Francis Grevemberg. These alone would make the book interesting to non-St. Landrians, but in addition, the book abounds in colorful and off-color anecdotes about Cat — all of his own making — that will bring a chuckle even to that rarity among Louisianians — someone who's never heard of Cat Doucet.

When a reporter asked Cat for comment on a newsstory that there was prostitution in St. Landry, the sheriff's reply was, in effect, that a little indulgence in the game of "beast with two backs" was never known to be physically harmful to its participants, except that it was less elegantly phrased. (Margaret's was a bordello on Church St. where joy reigned unrefined for 47 rollicking, profit-packed years until Francis Grevemberg, superintendent of state police who later ran for governor, padlocked it in 1957.)

They tell of the time when Cat's attention was called to the high cost of illicit love at such maisons de joie as Margaret's. The sheriff agreed, and suggested that perhaps for college boys and other low-income patrons, "they ought to fix it like at the restaurants; you know, like a child's plate."

Some stories are grim. The sheriff once ordered the body of a runaway murderer put on display, in the casket, in the Opelousas courthouse for three days so that all could see that the murderer had finally been apprehended. There is also a graphic, moving account of the last hanging at the gallows of criminals, complete with description of a preacher's blood-spattered clothes.

What Samuel Goldwyn was to Hollywood with his Goldwynisms ("Include me out"), Cat Doucet was to his constituents. His malapropisms are classic, and what Huey Long did purposely —

mutilate the English language to ingratiate himself with an illiterate audience — Cat did without having to try. "I'm gonna win big!" he shouted at a wildly cheering crowd during a campaign speech, "I'm gonna win by a landscape!"

On another occasion, the sixth grade-educated sheriff said of his opponent, "When he makes a speech, he has all kinds of things wrote down, and he reads that to you. Now me, when I talk, I talk out of my head."

Cat Doucet was reactionary, but in some respects he was progressive. Blacks were voting in St. Landry when other parishes were still fighting Negro registration tooth and nail. His enemies contend that Cat couldn't have cared less about civil rights, that he was interested only in the vote. This is the old quid pro quo of politics, you scratch my back and I'll scratch yours, and Cat was a master of the game.

Earl Long prided himself on being the last of the red-hot papas. Cat Doucet, until a stroke laid him low, was no mean dispenser, either, of sauce piquante in the political potpourri of his parish. He is among the last of the old pols-Louisiana style — and in "The Cat and St. Landry," Mary Alice Fontenot captures the style and personality of this fast-disappearing political breed in exceeding fine fashion, including the judicious use of many excellent photographs and sketches.

— Vincent Marino, editor
Lafayette Daily Advertiser

1

The Second Son

Imperial St. Landry: "mother of parishes," proving ground for statesmen, ethnic jambalaya. From the beginning a sauce piquante of politics, seasoned with fiery oratory, spiced with invective and caustic humor.

St. Landry, named for St. Landri, Bishop of Paris in 651, was once the governmental and cultural center of a vast area stretching from the Atchafalaya to the Sabine Rivers. From it, starting in 1840, were carved the parishes of Calcasieu, Cameron, Acadia, Evangeline, Allen, Beauregard and Jefferson Davis.

In its dim past St. Landry was the habitat of Indians; first, those fierce warriors, the Attakapas; then the Opelousas, Choctaw and Alabamans. Then came the white men — the French, the Spanish, the exiled Acadians, a sprinkling of Anglo-Saxons and other nationalities. Many acquired vast land grants, learned how to best utilize the fertile soil. They built fine plantation homes, bought many slaves, became wealthy and influential.

The sons of these pioneers — educated, polished, cultured — became doctors, lawyers, jurists and politicians as well as planters. These constituted the ruling families of the parish.

The poorer classes, which included many of the impoverished Acadians, free men of color and freed slaves, were largely dependent upon the land for a livelihood. Some were small farmers, others tenant farmers. They were, for the most part, unpolished and uneducated, with French as their only language.

Into this environment, on November 8, 1899, was born one Daly Joseph Doucet, who was to become the most colorful and controversial political figure the parish has yet to produce.

This is the story of his public life, gleaned from newspaper accounts of his career as sheriff for 20 years, from people who know him well, and from the man himself.

The second of the three sons of Lucius Doucet and Aza Lafleur Doucet, Daly Joseph was named for Dr. Lawrence Daly, a well known physician. Not because Dr. Daly was the family doctor, as was so often the case, but prophetically enough, because the doctor was also a politician. Lucius Doucet heard the name during a political campaign, liked it, and gave it to his second son.

The second name, Joseph, was his "saint name." The predominantly French-Acadian inhabitants of the area are also predominantly Catholic. Traditionally, when an infant is christened in the Catholic faith, if the name chosen by the parents is not the name of a saint or a derivative thereof, the name of a saint is added. This religious custom is followed punctiously by the descendants of the Louisiana Acadians.

Daly Joseph was born at Grand Prairie, in a house his father built, on land inherited from his grandfather, Lastie Doucet. Grand Prairie, or "Big Prairie," is a rural settlement, not an incorporated town. A cotton gin, a Catholic church, a school, a few country stores and a scattering of farm houses constitute the community, situated some 12 miles northwest of Opelousas, the parish seat.

Lastie Doucet, Daly Joseph's grandfather, owned some 1,500 arpents of land on the prairie, which was eventually divided among his five sons: Clopha, Theo, Frank, Regile and Lucius. The Doucet brothers all built homes along the public road a short distance from each other. Their children grew up together.

When Lucius Doucet and Aza Lafleur were first married, they lived in the original Doucet home which had been built by Lastie. This typically Acadian house was of "bousillage" construction: the walls of sawed lumber daubed on the inside with mud and Spanish moss. This primitive insulation — to be had for free — provided warmth against the damp, chilly cold of Louisiana winters, and coolness during the torrid summers.

The youngest of Lastie's sons and his bride lived here until their own place could be built, which was accomplished in the manner of the times, by a "coup de main," a helping hand, from relatives and neighbors.

Lucius and Aza's house, consisting of two bedrooms and a kitchen, was also of Acadian architecture but without the mud-daubed walls: a high, steep-pitched roof, built-in front porch with an outside stairway leading to the attic. The house, fronted by oak trees planted by Lucius, still stands at Grand Prairie. It now has glass window panes and window screens instead of the wooden shutters of the original structure, and another room has been added. Otherwise it is the same.

The eldest of the Lucius Doucet sons, Hosea, was three and a half years older than Daly Joseph. The youngest, Elton, is two years younger. The fourth child and only girl in the family, Vivian, died at age three. The little girl suffered a fractured hip when she fell from a swing; a fatal infection developed. The Doucets also lost another child, a son, soon after birth.

The life style of the Doucets, like that of most country people of the early 20th century, contrasted sharply with the elegant life enjoyed by the more affluent planters of the region.

Water came from a hand pump in the back yard and from rain barrels. The family bathtub was a lard barrel, cut in half, the ingrained grease burned out with corn shucks. During the summer the boys bathed in cold water; in winter, Aza built a roaring fire in the kitchen stove, heated a huge kettle of water and kept the fire going while her shivering sons took turns scrubbing down in the sawed-off barrel.

Keeping a supply of firewood on hand was a year 'round job; the wood was needed for cooking as well as heating. Daly Joseph and his brothers helped Lucius cut the firewood in the nearby woods and haul it in by wagon. The boys would stack the wood in neat cords in the back yard, handy for Aza to bring in an armload for her kitchen stove, and in winter, for both the stove and fireplace.

The humid summers brought swarms of mosquitoes from the low lying swampy areas. Mosquito bars over the beds kept the pests at bay, for sleeping, also kept out whatever cooling breezes that might come in through the opened doors and window shutters. Between dusk and bedtime, the boys built fires in the yard to create smoke to drive away the stinging insects. After the fire got going good, some moist wood or Spanish moss was piled on the flames and a thick, pungent smoke ensued.

Daly Joseph became "Cat" almost before he could talk.

The way he acquired the unique nickname is a story that Cat has told many times, usually in answer to the inevitable question asked by reporters. He always tells it the same way; now, because

3

of shortness of breath since he developed emphyesma, he uses fewer words, shorter sentences:

"When I was two-three years old, a stray cat came to the house. My brother Hosea and my cousin Ned Doucet — they was older than me — they got me to go under the house and catch the cat. I caught him. The cat bit me. Bit my hand, and I got blood poison.

"My old mama had to drive to Washington in a horse and buggy two-three times a week for the doctor to treat me. I couldn't talk good. I was too young. When they would say, 'what's the matter with your hand?' I would say in French, 'chat'! Cat, you see. And that's how I got the name."

Another person — a long-time Doucet deputy who eventually got fired for disloyalty — has a different version of how the nickname originated. Lucius Doucet's brother, Theo, owned a large general store in Grand Prairie, a landmark in the community. The story goes that once the store was entered and some trifling amount of goods — a pocket knife and some candy — was taken. When the loss was discovered, it was determined that entry into the store had been made through the narrow transom over the front door. Someone made the observation: "Only a cat could have climbed up there and got in!"

Suspicion, the story continues, fell on Daly Joseph, one of the few individuals around small enough to have climbed through the transom, and the only one of the Doucet clan believed to be *"canaille"* enough to do such a thing. Uncle Theo discounted the idea that one of his own nephews, even Daly, could be a petty thief. Nonetheless, the name "Cat" stuck.

There is little doubt that the story was fabricated, like so many of the stories circulated about D. J. "Cat" Doucet. In the first place, there was no transom above the door at the Theo Doucet store. There were only two doors — both of wood — one at the front and one at the back, the back door giving easy assess to the adjacent residence. There were wooden shutters at the windows. The doors and windows were well secured with strong locks at the close of each day's business. Unlikely that a small boy could break and enter such a place.

4

Aza never called her son "Cat." All of her life she called him Daly, which she pronounced "Day-lay," the Acadian way.

The nickname was a fighting word to young Daly. He was constantly teased about the *"p'tit nom,"* and this triggered fights and feuds among the younger members of the Doucet family. His resentment carried over into his school days, and many were the noses bloodied.

Cat no longer minds being called Cat. The name is part of his image. He's proud of it. The name is uniquely his. Where else in Louisiana — perhaps in the entire South — is there another Cat?

Lucius Doucet was a cotton and corn farmer, planting some 150 acres. At the time the boys were growing up, cotton was four and five cents a pound. But whatever the price of cotton, this was a frugal family, making do with what they had, saving pennies, buying only the necessities.

The Doucet boys worked early and late in the fields, chopping weeds in the cotton rows, picking cotton at harvest time. They were in the fields by daybreak, working until time to change clothes, grab a bite of breakfast — usually cornbread and milk — and walk the mile and a half to the Grand Prairie school. After school, it was change back into work clothes and return to the fields until dark.

Food came from the garden and barnyard. The few items of staple groceries that had to be bought were purchased with eggs laid by Aza's hens. The clothes the boys wore were made by their mother.

School wasn't too popular with Cat. Over the years, Lucius and Aza learned to speak some English, but at the time their sons were in school only French was spoken in the Doucet home. The boys started school knowing not one word of English.

"My first teacher was Paul Pavy," said Cat. "We called him Prof. Pavy. Not any of the children at school could talk English. Prof. Pavy passed a rule that nobody could speak French on the school grounds.

"At recess we played marbles like we were deef and dumb. Without saying a word. We couldn't talk English, and were

5

scared to talk French because we would be punished."

The teacher's rule was respected, and in time, appreciated. "That's the only way we could have learned English," says Cat.

The ruling that banned the speaking of French on school grounds was not confined to the Grand Prairie school. This was the general practice at schools in all French-speaking communities; it was a matter of expediency. The pupils were growing up in an increasingly English-oriented world; the teachers, for the most part, spoke only English, the text books were in English.

So, like it or not, Cat Doucet and all other French-Acadian school children learned to speak English. In Cat's case, it wasn't exactly the King's English, but he absorbed enough to survive in the jungle of Louisiana politics.

Cat despised going to school, and used every excuse to keep from going to class. It wasn't easy to "play hooky." There were no streets, no alleyways, no vacant buildings in which a rebellious schoolboy could while away the day. Only the wide open prairie and the public road, where exposure to one of the numerous Doucet relatives was practically inevitable.

But play hooky Cat did, in company with a school buddy known as "Caro" Fontenot, who also grew up to be a peace officer. Walking to school, each carrying lunch packed in a tin syrup bucket, the boys would sneak into the cemetery near the church and spend the day playing behind the tombstones. When they got hungry they would open up the lunch buckets, which usually contained cold biscuits or cornbread spread with cane syrup, and fried sausage or *"p'tit sale"* (salted down pork).

When the other children would come trudging back down the road, kicking up the thick dust or jumping mud puddles as the case might be, Cat and Caro would join the homeward-bound procession, daring the other kids to open their mouths.

The social life of the community centered around the church and the Theo Doucet store. On Sundays, farm families visited with each other before and after the one Mass, said by the priest from the Washington church who rode the six miles on horseback. The store, typical of country stores of that era, had a porch across the front on which were several home-made cowhide bottom chairs. Boards secured between the porch posts served as benches; the posts were convenient hitching racks for horses. During the week farmers drove their wives in buggies or wagons to the store, sat on the porch and talked crops or politics while the women bought wares within.

There were also the traditional Cajun social activities, common in all areas settled by the French-Acadians: the *"fais-do-do,"* the *"boucherie,"* weddings and funerals, and of course the *"veillée,"* informal visiting with neighbors and friends between supper and bedtime.

Lucius and Aza went to some of the weddings, all of the funerals they could get to, and did a modest amount of visiting. The couple was not much given to frivolity; they did little dancing after they were married, left the *"fais-do-do"* to their unmarried friends. As for the *"boucheries,"* these were family affairs. Since the five Doucet brothers lived so near each other, each would take a turn butchering a hog or a calf and share the meat with the other four families.

Recalling his boyhood in Grand Prairie, the "old sheriff," as he has come to be known in the parish, remembered some of the incidents of his youth.

Once he fell into the underground cistern on the place. He was playing on top of the cistern, which extended a couple of feet above ground, and the wooden cover caved in.

"There was six-seven feet of water in there," Cat related. "Elton was six weeks old. I was two. And I was just getting over pneumonia. My old mother, she had just had that new baby, she jumped in there to get me."

Aza managed to slide a plank into the cistern, and with this was able to hold the boy's head above water while five-year-old Hosea ran the half mile to the home of an uncle, Clopha Doucet, to get help.

"I don't remember that, but I remember them telling about it," said Cat. "And about the time one of the uncles pulled me out of the bayou, half drowned. It had rained a lot. The bayou was high. There's where we used to swim. I was showing off. I

7

couldn't swim so good then, and I was trying to do like my older cousins."

With a dozen-plus young cousins to aid and abet, Cat and his brothers found it easy to get into mischief. Once several of the boys, with Cat as ringleader, tied a 20-shot roman candle onto a dog's back and lit the fireworks. The terrified animal, with the roman candle spewing balls of fire in all directions, ran under the barn and into a thick litter of dry corn shucks. The shucks caught fire, of course. It took the entire Doucet clan to put out the flames, which threatened to destroy the barn.

The story that Aza liked best to tell was about the time Cat had a fight with a girl. Probably because this was his mother's favorite story of his childhood, and told it often, details of the incident remain fresh in Cat's memory today.

"Her name was Rowena Whitley," Cat recalled. "I had a bunch of fights with her. She used to devil me all the time!"

The feud started one day when Cat was wearing a new hat his mother had just bought for him.

"We was walking home from school. Rowena took my hat and pitched it in the cherokees. You know, them wild rose bushes with stickers — the farmers used to let 'em grow high for a fence to keep the cattle in. My hat stayed up there and I couldn't get it. So I pulled Rowena's hair and she pushed me in the ditch."

Cat arrived home with his school clothes all wet and muddy, and no hat. Aza demanded an explanation, then gave him a good whipping. "To teach you not to fight with girls!" she said.

Several days later Cat and Rowena got into it again. This time he pushed her in the ditch.

The little girl's older sister went to the Doucet home to report on the incident, apparently seeking retribution. But Aza had her own idea of justice. No, she said. "I whipped him the first time he and Rowena had a fight. This time I think Rowena should get the whipping."

As a youngster, Cat kept goats. He himself doesn't remember how many he had; "two-three, I guess." A cousin, Belle Doucet

8

Martin, reminisced about Cat and the animals:

"Those goats used to follow Cat around Grand Prairie just like the politicians used to follow him around the courthouse!"

Cat had goats from the time he was old enough to care for pets. "And everywhere that Cat went, the goats followed," Belle said. Belle's folks, the Regile Doucets, lived a short distance from Lucius and Aza.

"I can still see Cat coming down the road with three or four goats following him," said Belle. "My mother would say: *'ferme la porte, vite!'* close the door, quick! 'Cat's coming with his goats!'"

With the unscreened doors open in summer, the goats would follow Cat in the house, jump on beds, knock over furniture and butt indiscriminately.

"Poor Tante Aza!" Belle continued. "She had a time with that boy and his goats. I can still hear her fussing when the goats would jump on her clean beds. 'Day-lay,' she would say sternly 'get those goats out of here, Day-lay!'"

Belle prefaced and ended her story with: "That Cat! He always was a devil!"

Real trouble resulted the time the Doucet boys played, literally, with dynamite.

In some manner Lucius had acquired some dynamite caps, and had stored them in the house in an old *"armoire."* The way Cat tells the story, his older brother Hosea played the lead role in this little drama, and ended up by losing two of his fingers.

"Hosea was fooling around in the *armoire* and he found them dynamite caps," Cat said. "We didn't know it was dynamite. I guess we didn't even know what dynamite was. Hosea took a hatpin — the long kind that ladies used to pin their hats on their hairs — and stuck it in the dynamite cap, and it exploded in his hand. It's a wonder it didn't blow his head off — and mine too! Dr. Lazaro — the old man, Ladie's papa — he came and cut his two fingers off."

That's all Cat had to say about that, but relating the incident apparently triggered another memory of school days in Grand

9

The Cat and St. Landry

Prairie and uncovered another bit of deviltry:

"Miss Mildred Splane was one of the teachers at the school. She used to drive to school in a horse and buggy from the old Splane place, five-six miles. She'd let us unhitch her horse, and hitch 'im up again when school was out. We'd let her get started, then we would hop on the back of the buggy and steal a ride. Sometimes she'd find out, and switch us with her buggy whip!"

2

Mr. Malaprop

Politics has always been the dominant factor in Cat Doucet's life. "That's all I know," he says. "I've been in politics all my life."

Lucius Doucet was a ward constable; also a member of a large and influential family that could deliver the votes. The Doucet home was a gathering place for parish politicians, particularly during a campaign.

"Lee Garland and Henry Lastrapes, they used to come spend the night at the house," Cat said. "They would come in a buggy and talk politics with my daddy. It would be too late to drive the 12 miles back to Opelousas, especially when it was bad weather, so they would stay spend the night."

(Lee Garland, member of one of the ruling families of the parish, was district attorney at the time Huey Long gerrymandered Garland and Judge Benjamin Pavy out of office. Henry Lastrapes, long-time clerk of court, was one of the most respected political figures of his time).

"I'll never forget that," Cat said. "One time old man Henry give me two nickels. It was the first money I ever had. He gave each of us nickels."

The two men spent many nights at the Doucet residence. Cat would sit quietly on the floor and listen to the talk. It was the boys' job to keep the fireplace stoked with wood. As the night wore on and still the talk went on, the brothers would yawn sleepily and go to bed; Cat stayed, listening avidly to everything that was said.

The Lucius Doucet family moved to Ville Platte when Cat was 3. Evangeline Parish, the last division of Imperial St. Landry, had just been created, and Ville Platte was the parish seat.

"My old mother wanted us to get a good education.. That's the reason we moved," Cat said.

A half century ago, the French-speaking Acadians considered

that anyone who could read and write had "a good education." Such a person held the respect of his peers. Despite the fact that most Acadians of the time believed education of little value, the pressures of the times were upon them. They couldn't know that their isolation as an ethnic group was fast coming to an end. They did realize that it gave community status when families did not have to go to outsiders to get their few letters read and answered, business documents translated, or figures added or subtracted.

Cat never doubted that he got that "good education" Proudly he says: "I went to the sixth grade." He used that scanty schooling for all it was worth, and ended up as Louisiana's most noted — and most quoted — Mr. Malaprop.

For almost 40 years, since he became a public figure, people have collected his word blunders like gems, to be exhibited whenever and wherever there is an appreciative audience.

And there's always an appreciative audience in St. Landry; the magic words are: "Did you hear the latest one about Cat?"

Hearing these "bijoux" in a Cat Doucet anecdote, friends and foes howl with delight. Friends say "that's Cat for you! Nobody else could have said that!" Foes, savoring the item for use against him, exclaim: "Imagine a guy who said a thing like that getting elected!"

The probable truth of the matter is: he did not become a successful politician despite his public assassination of the English language, but because of it.

The Cat's English is definitely not the King's English. Nor was the King's English meaningful to those sons of the Acadians who were his constituents. To these, who constituted the majority of voters in the 1930's, English was the "foreign" language.

When Cat got up on the courthouse square or on radio to make a campaign speech, his supporters were certain one thing: they would be able to understand everything he said. Because this bilingual native of the big prairie spoke their language, French. And when he repeated his speech in English for the benefit of *"les Americains,"* they applauded wildly when he stated:

"Mais yes, I'm going to win! I'm going to win by a landscape!"
Or:

"My friends, you know my opponent. When he makes a speech, he has all kinds of things written down, and he reads that to you. Now me, when I talk, I talk out of my head!"

No matter what ridicule the punch line of this story might bring from a professor of English, to Cat's supporters this was proof of achievement, something that added to the stature of their candidate. They knew what he meant.

It didn't matter when more literate hearers pointed up these economy-size blunders. The Cajun voters also had trouble finding the right words in English. The difference was, most were too embarassed to use their broken English; but *"le Chat,"* he had the guts to do it, and before a crowd at that.

In time, friends and foes came to realize the publicity value of Cat's misuse of English. The mistakes he made were remembered, repeated, talked about for weeks, months, years.

His detractors even charged that he made such mistakes on purpose, for effect. Such was not the case. Cat's word blunders were — and still are — the honest mistakes of a person seeking to communicate in an alien language.

The Doucets lived in the town of Ville Platte, within easy walking distance of Sacred Heart School, where Aza sent her sons to be educated. Cat's few years in the town had no great impact on his boyhood memories, except for his exploits with his dog, Woodrow Wilson:

"One of my uncles, Frank Doucet, gave me a bulldog by the name of Woodrow Wilson. There were not many bulldogs when I was a young boy, 13-14 years old. I made Woodrow Wilson fight all the dogs in Ville Platte!"

The Cat and Woodrow Wilson got in bad with the Ville Platte chief of police, Hilaire "Boo-Boo" Vidrine.

"The people from the country would come to town in wagons and buggies, and their dogs would follow. When I'd see a dog, I'd whistle for my bulldog. The mules would kick, sometimes the horses would run away with the wagon — scared by the fighting around their feet."

He chuckled. "I gave 'em a bad time with my dog. Of course

13

Woodrow Wilson would always win. But the chief, he would get mad at me. You know, for creating a disturbance.

"To pay the chief back all the devil I gave him — years after, he got to be a game warden. Huey Long appointed him. And I was a game warden, appointed by Huey. Hilaire, he didn't know how to read and write. So I'd make out his report for him, and I showed his little daughter how to make out his report, so he could get his expenses back. I used to tell him, 'I'm paying you back for all the devil I gave you with Woodrow Wilson!'"

When Cat was 17 he tried to enlist in the United States Army.

"I went to New Orleans to join the army," he said. "I wanted to enlist before I was 18 — it was the first World War, and I knew I was going to get drafted."

Hosea, the elder brother, had been drafted despite the two missing fingers.

"They didn't take me," Cat continued. "I was rejected. I had a flat foot. I was flat footed. They wanted to operate — make an operation on me. I wouldn't agree to that; I wasn't suffering!

"We went four-five from Ville Platte, boys my age. They all passed but me. George Vidrine, he got killed in Germany. And there was Philo Chapman, he's another buddy of mine, we were all raised together in Ville Platte. He passed. I failed."

In New Orleans Cat learned that the government was employing men to serve as guards at a munitions plant in Alabama. He signed up for the job, and for the first time left the state of Louisiana.

With other employes of the United States government, Cat traveled in a special coach from New Orleans to Muscle Shoals, Alabama, to work as a guard at a powder plant on the Tennessee River, located between Sheffield and Florence, Alabama. "I guess they kept us there about a year," he said.

Cat remembers the place was like an oil boom town, "with lots of strange people walking all over." His pay was $150 a month, quite a handsome salary in those days.

"They gave us a confederal uniform and a confederal hat, a holster and a pistol to guard the plant. All the guards were commissioned deputies."

The guards took full advantage of their position and authority,

14

using their deputy commissions to gain free admission into the shows and circuses that came to town.

"We'd walk in for nothing and take up all the seats. We were about four-five hundred guards. The show people would holler, but there was nothing they could do!"

Three days after Cat's 19th birthday the Armistice was signed. The war was over, and he had not been drafted.

The post-war years found Cat experimenting with ways of making a living.

"It took me a while to get started," he said. "I used to drive a transfer in Opelousas. We didn't call them taxis in those days. We called them transfers.

"Me and Onezime Wyble and Ryan Thompson — Ryan, he had a double team on his hack, he'd meet drummers at the depot. He kept his horses at Remi Wallior's stable, where the American Department Store is now. There was another livery stable that Dr. Haas owned, right on the corner by the Coca-Cola plant on Court Street."

He went off on a brief tangent, remembering that at that time the principal streets in Opelousas were surfaced with wooden blocks.

"Every time it would rain hard the blocks would float away. They'd have to catch 'em and put 'em back."

The older transfer drivers used horse-drawn vehicles. Cat drove a Model-T Ford, later bought himself a small Overland.

"We used to meet the trains, me and Wyble and Ryan, and bring the drummers to the James Hotel, where the Planter's Bank is now. It had been the Lacombe Hotel. Mr. Adam Budd owned it. Mr. Budd had a grandson by the name of James and the boy died. So he changed the name of the hotel to the James Hotel.

"I used to drive the drummers around. They had their sample cases. I'd take them to stores in the country — Prairie Ronde, Grand Prairie, and to Leon Wolff's store in Washington. Did I tell you I bought my first pair of long pants at Leon Wolff's store?"

The traveling salesmen liked Opelousas, Cat recalled. For those inclined to fun and games, the town had plenty to offer.

"They didn't have any trouble finding women," said Cat. "Carlton — that's what they called the red light district — was right out there," he waved an expansive hand. "And it was full of public women and fancy-foot gals. There were from 10 to 15 houses with public women."

He proceeded to name some of the notorious "madams" of the day, and the location of the houses.

"I couldn't go in," he added. "I was too young. I'd sit in my transfer and wait for the men."

In addition to driving the drummers to the "cat houses" and on their country rounds, Cat the transfer man also earned fees for out-of-town trips from Opelousas residents.

"Used to charge $3 to drive to Ville Platte. Gasoline was 15 cents a gallon. I would drive Mr. Johnny Lewis or Raoul Pavy. They had lots of law practice in Ville Platte. If I had to stay all day they would give me $5 for the trip."

He digressed briefly to relate an incident connected with the establishment of Ville Platte as the seat of the newly created Evangeline Parish:

"I was there when they dedicated the new courthouse, in 1913," he said. "My daddy had a derrick which he used for well digging. He was the one that set the courthouse cornerstone with his derrick.

"I'll never forget — Rene Derouen, the one who became congressman — he was president of the Evangeline Bank then — he took some money and marked it with his initials, R.L.D. I don't remember if it was a dime or a quarter — maybe it was a silver dollar — but it's still in that cornerstone."

It was probably during his transfer-driving days that Cat and his cousin, Marshall Doucet, made a trip to New Orleans. The cousins took an "excursion" to the city. An excursion was a train trip of brief duration, usually 24 hours, at a ridiculously low fare, perhaps a dollar or two for the round trip. Excursions to New Orleans were available at various times, especially for the Mardi Gras, and were widely advertised in the newspapers. Cajun youths from throughout the bayou country would save up to board an excursion for a fling in the big city. The coaches on the excursion train were usually filled to capacity.

The trip to New Orleans required little more than the fare. Entertainment was for free; just being there, gawking at the crowds and sights, was enough. No one ever thought of sleeping once in the city and food was no problem. A good meal before leaving home and a sandwich in the city would suffice. And at the French Market one might buy a bunch of bananas, an entire stem from the banana plant containing more than a hundred of the fruit, for 50 cents. It was common practice for country passengers to buy a bunch of bananas to take home on the train and munch on along the way, still have plenty left to share with the folks at home.

A bunch of bananas was quite a load to haul the approximate mile from the market to Union Station, even for a husky country youth. Some of the banana buyers would pack the bananas on their backs, others would drag the bunch along the street with a length of twine. Once in the crowded coach the next problem would be where to put the bananas.

When Cat and Marshall entered the coach for the return trip, each packing a bunch of bananas, Marshall found a seat but Cat did not. The one seat left was occupied by a pair of shoes. A tired passenger had taken off his shoes and placed them on the seat, obstensibly to keep the seat free so he could stretch out and sleep during the five-hour ride home.

Cat was foot-weary himself. After a while he got tired of standing in the aisle and holding on to his bananas.

"That's somebody's place?" he inquired, pointing to the seat occupied by the shoes.

"Nope," said the passenger. He made no move to remove the shoes.

"Did you pay for that seat?"

"Nope," was the answer. "But I'm going to keep it anyway."

With that Cat picked up the fellow's shoes and pitched them out the window of the moving train.

This precipitated a ruckus in the coach. The shoeless passenger was irate, of course, and several of the other passengers were about to get into the act when the conductor intervened and threatened

17

to put all participants off the train.

"I guess it wasn't funny to that fellow," said Marshall, who contributed the anecdote. "But we sure did laugh when he got off at Lafayette and started walking down the street in his socks!"

Working at an out-of-state munitions plant, making excursion trips, driving a taxi — this was enough, in the 1920's, to put a veneer of sophistication on a young Cajun. Cat had been around.

Consequently, when two of his less-experienced friends needed his services, he was ready, willing and able.

"It was me that took them two boys to Atlanta. Meus Lafleur, he was from Basile, and Leo Soileau of Ville Platte. Meus and Leo, they played French music at the dances around here, and they wanted them to go to Atlanta to make a record.

"They gave us each $100. And our expenses. Those boys wouldn't go without me. You know them Cajuns wouldn't go to no big city like Atlanta by theirselves. I loaned Meus one of my suits.

"And we went first class. Stayed at one of the biggest hotels in Atlanta. I had told those people we didn't want to be put up at no joint. And we went on the train and had sleepers."

Cat doesn't remember just how he got in on the act, but speculated it was because he had been driving the two musicians around in his taxi to play at dances.

"The man from RCA — I believe it was RCA — that record company that had the sign with the little dog listening to the big horn — he came and talked to me, and we arranged that I would go over there with Meus and Leo. Meus, he's dead now, but Leo, he's still living in Ville Platte, last I heard.

"I know *'Jolie Blonde'* was one of the tunes they recorded. Another one was *'Mamma, Where You At,'* and *'Grand Basile'* and *'Valse Misère'* too.

"I was real young then, but I don't remember the year. But I know it was during Prohibition. We had a problem with the boys. They were used to having a drink or two before they would play, some of that good bootleg stuff people around here used to make.

"Well, they didn't have nothing like that in Georgia. It was a dry state.

18

"Those boys just couldn't get going. Leo played the violin, and Meus played the accordion and he would sing. They couldn't get started.

"So I went to a drug store and got some alcohol, 190 proof, and I made them put something in it, strawberry syrup or something like that.

"After two-three pops of that, they cranked off!"

Thus Cat Doucet played a big part in getting the first Cajun music record produced. This record is now a collector's item.

It was along about this time that Cat was also a boxing promoter.

"That was in Lafayette," he said. "There was a boxing arena right back of the Evangeline Hotel. Lionel Jeanmard and Lee Burke, who used to be a railroad clerk, they were in on the deal.

"We had some good fighters, too. K. O. White of Opelousas, he fought a long time then he went to Chicago and never came back. He was a brother to 'Doc' White, that fellow that's been at the Daily World so long.

"And we had Chris Achten of Eunice. And Johnny McCoy from Crowley. His name was Hoffpauir, but he called himself McCoy. There was a Dr. Montgomery — the one that had the drug store — on the boxing commission."

Cat doesn't remember why he decided to give up being a transfer man. "I guess I got tired of it," he said. He tried his hand at being an automobile salesman. His new job was in Crowley, the seat of Acadia Parish.

The car dealer, Larry Hollier, was also a farm implement dealer. Part of Cat's job was to demonstrate a tractor designed especially for use on marshy terrain. Potential customers were the rice farmers in the Florence area south of Gueydan.

"I was right at home with them fellows," Cat said. "They all spoke French, and I got along good. But I didn't sell no tractors. They cost too much money."

When he was 21 Cat found himself a wife — a demure, dark-haired Acadian beauty, Anna Dorcey. Anna was the daughter of a Lafayette barber, Alphonse Dorcey. Her mother died when Anna

19

was quite young and her father re-married. The step-mother had some strong convictions about how a young girl should be raised. Anna wasn't allowed to go out alone with Cat during their courtship.

"The old lady made me park my car in front of the house and leave it there," Cat said. "Then she would let me and Anna walk to the picture show. But not by ourselves. We had to take one of her little sisters or brothers."

Anna and Cat were married in the Cathedral of St. John the Evangelist, in Lafayette. The officiating priest was Father William Teurlings, the same priest who had baptized Cat and given him First Communion.

(Like many St. Landrians, Cat has fond memories of this European priest. Father Teurlings, a native of Holland, came to the Washington church as pastor in 1899, the year Cat was born, and it was he who rode horseback to Grand Prairie to say Mass at the mission church. Some years later he was appointed pastor of the Lafayette church parish. During his pastorate the structure that is now the cathedral was built, also St. Genevieve's Church of Lafayette, which he served as pastor until his death in 1957)

Cat tried two more occupations: barbering, like his father-in-law, and working for the railroad.

"I went to New Orleans to Russell Barber College. To get experience, we would have to shave old tramps and people like that, for 10 cents. Them fellows that came on the boats, they had beards like the hippies do now. I'd have to put the clippers on their faces before I could use the razor."

After completing the barbering course, he went to Eunice and bought himself a barber shop.

"Howard McManus owned the shop. He wanted to retire. The shop had belonged to Mr. Johnson, Vic Johnson's papa. Howard bought it from Mr. Johnson, I bought it from Howard. Mr. Johnson would come in and help me on Wednesdays and Saturdays. His customers were the old men of the town. They were used to the way he cut their hairs and shaved them.

"I had to shave them old men, they had hard beards and I couldn't keep my razor sharp. That's what discouraged me from barbering. So I quit that."

Cat's try at becoming a railroad man never came off.

"Lafayette had a big roundhouse. I wanted to be a switchman. So I went there to see the chief clerk. Let's see if I can remember his name."

A long pause ensued while he prodded his memory back over the 50-year-plus span. "I think his name was Mealey. Yeah. That was it, Mealey."

According to railroad company rules, an apprentice switchman had to work for a period of two weeks wihout pay, then take an examination before being hired.

"I did this student work for the two weeks. Nothing happened. I worked into the third week, then I went to meet Mr. Mealey. I explained I was ready for the examination, that I was married and couldn't keep on working for nothing."

But the chief clerk put him off. He told Cat to come back another time.

"After he told me two-three times that he didn't have time to fool with me, I told him to take his railroad and go to the devil!

"And that was the end of my railroad career."

That was also the end of his search for fame and fortune outside of St. Landry Parish.

Cat and Anna moved to Opelousas. Meanwhile his parents and two brothers had also moved from Ville Platte to Opelousas.

It was here that their six children were born. Alberta, the first born, was premature and weighed but three and a half pounds at birth.

"It was my old mother saved her," Cat said. "She fed that little baby with a medicine dropper. They didn't have no big hospitals and incubators, things like that."

Aza was also the officiating *"mère-mère"* when the other five children were born.

"We lived in a little house back of the Dudley Guilbeau place," Cat reminisced. "Dr. Albert Pavy, he waited on my wife for our first three kids, Alberta, Harold and Yvonne. At home. In those days they didn't haul 'em to the hospital and start giving 'em shots nine months in advance!

"Dr. Pavy used to smoke Prince Albert tobacco. He'd roll his own cigarettes. We'd make coffee all night, waiting for the baby to come. My old mother was there for every baby."

After Yvonne's birth there was an interval of 11 years, then the Doucets had another son, Louis Austin, named for L. Austin Fontenot Sr.

"I named him for old man Austin — he was like a daddy to me. Then we had Anna Dale, then Daly Joe Jr. Three girls, three boys. A girl and a boy, a girl and a boy, a girl and a boy, like that."

All of the children were sent to Catholic schools. The girls finished at the Academy of the Immaculate Conception, in Opelousas, and the boys at St. Stanislaus, Bay St. Louis, Mississippi.

3

Huey And "Mister Austin"

The first time Huey P. Long ran for governor of Louisiana, in 1924, he barely made a ripple in the St. Landry political pond.

The Opelousas newspaper, in an editorial published after the first primary election, endorsed Henry Fuqua for governor. Hewitt Bouanchard had been high man in the primary, the editorial reminded. The name of the third candidate, Huey Long, was mentioned only incidentally — when it was pointed out that he had polled a mere 674 votes in St. Landry.

Four years later, when Huey was staging his second campaign, he spoke at a rally on the Opelousas courthouse square. The newspaper devoted almost two columns of type, under a five-column headline on front page, to Huey's speech. The tone of the story was derisive:

"Not satisfied with ridiculing state departments, the candidate took a fling at local office holders and stated that holding office too long was injurious to the public welfare . . . Mr. Long could tell a joke that kept the crowd in gales of laughter from the time he started talking until he finished.

"Remarks heard throughout the crowd were to the effect that Commissioner Long was an excellent mimic and would have done much better as a showman than a candidate for governor."

No estimate was given on the number of persons attending the Long rally. Only "the crowd." The story indicated that "the crowd" had turned out for entertainment only; that it was inconceivable that anyone could take this joker seriously.

The Opelousas newspaper, one of two weeklies in the parish, had two obvious reasons for being anti-Long: Two native St. Landrians were in the running for the two highest offices in the state: gubernatorial candidate O. H. Simpson, who, as lieutenant governor had acceded to the governorship when Governor Henry Fuqua died in office, and Dr. F. Octave Pavy, running for lieutenant governor on the Simpson ticket.

The Cat and St. Landry

Twelve days before Huey won his overwhelming victory he rated two paragraphs — and an apology of sorts — on the bottom fold of front page. The one-column headline read:

"Huey Long Speaks to Small Crowd at Courthouse Sunday."

The story writer estimated that 150 persons had heard the speech, and added: "the crowd hearing him Sunday was said to be the smallest he had spoken to on his tour."

The second of the two paragraphs read as follows:

"As reported in the News last week, Mr. Long was to speak Monday night. This was a typographical error for which the News wishes to make correction. Mr. Long was scheduled to speak Sunday and not Monday as reported."

The newspaper was the only news media; the error could well have been responsible for the smallness of the crowd, whether or not made in good faith. But the belated correction was undoubtedly sternly demanded by Huey's first lieutenant in St. Landry — L. Austin Fontenot Sr., a brilliant attorney, astute politician, powerful friend and patron of D. J. "Cat" Doucet.

"I owe everything to Huey Long and Mister Austin," said Cat. "I was always a Long man. It was Huey that give me my first job, my first political job. He made me a game warden. And he did that because Old Man Austin asked him. He wasn't so old then, but I called him Old Man Austin because he had a son named Austin Jr. He was like my own daddy. I always listened to Mister Austin.

"The only time I didn't vote Long was when Earl ran when Huey didn't want him to. The first time I went to Huey's house with Old Man Austin, well, Russell was just a kid then.

"I'll never forget when I met Huey. It was at a meeting at the courthouse when he was running for governor the first time. There wasn't many people there. Huey said, 'I'm a Baptist, but that's no credit to the Baptist Church.' The way he said it, it was like he was one of us. He didn't win that time. But he went back and got in four years later.

"Huey used to say, 'I can run hell, but I can't run St. Landry.' And Earl and I were always close, except that time I didn't suport him. He came to Opelousas and stopped me in front of Shute's

Drug Store. He told me — I was running for sheriff then — he said: 'You ain't gonna win for sheriff, you'd better watch your game warden job because you're gonna lose it!'

"I told him, 'Earl, whenever you want your game warden job back you can have it.' He thought he was gonna be governor; trying to bluff me.

"And I said, 'let me tell you something, Earl. You ain't gonna be governor, and I'm gonna be sheriff. And that's how it came out. Other than that, Earl and me, we were always good friends."

Cat Doucet had good reason to be grateful that he had a job as game warden. He was the father of a growing family, and the Great Depression was upon the nation.

The local newspapers reflected the grim times:

A Church Point bank failed to open; a Eunice bank closed its doors. One issue of the paper reported three suicides; the sale of marriage licenses was at a record low, stated Clerk of Court Henry Lastrapes.

Judge Ben C. Dawkins, presiding in federal court in Opelousas, fined 62 of the 150 persons charged with violations of the liquor prohibition law.

And for every violator caught, one might safely surmise that three other bootleggers got away. Just about everybody violated the law when it came to alcoholic beverages. Except for a minority — a handful of people in the parish with strong anti-liquor convictions — just about everybody had a few bottles of homemade blackberry wine in the pantry, or a crock of beer brewing on the back porch.

And many of the "have-nots" — country people who had lost their farms, town people without jobs — took to distilling hard liquor and selling it to buy necessities for their families.

Doing so put these otherwise honest people in the same category with chronic lawbreakers and the big money bootleggers. Their names on the federal court docket created stigmas that their families haven't been able to live down yet. And, as is usually the case, those who point the finger are the erstwhile customers.

There are those who say that these violations of the unpopular

18th Amendment were what saved the economy of the parish during the depression. St. Landry moonshine had a state-wide repute; college men coming home for the weekend brought two suitcases — one filled with clothes for mama to launder, the other empty to bring back "Opelousas corn" for the fellows in the dorm.

Cat Doucet has been accused of being a bootlegger, during the years before he became a game warden. If so, he was one of those who got away with it. His name did not appear on any of the federal court dockets.

He denies the charge.

"No, I never did do that. But I'll tell you what I did do. There was a fellow in Leonville who made real good whiskey, the best you could buy in St. Landry Parish. I used to go over there and buy five gallons at a time, in a wooden keg. I'd bring it to Shreveport. It was for a United States marshal. He drank a lot. He had me do that for a long time.

"I knew I was taking a big chance. Of course I wasn't sheriff then, or a deputy. I don't know what I would have done if the federal agents would have stopped me and searched the car. I told the marshal if ever they did that I was going to say the whiskey was for him. He said, 'I don't care. Just get me that whiskey!'"

Cat's game warden job paid $75 a month. "Plus 10 or 15 cents a mile for my car."

This was a scant living, even during the depression years.

He managed to line up a couple of part-time occupations, both of a political nature, to supplement his meager salary.

"Johnny Healey was secretary-treasurer of the police jury for a long time. He was a friend of mine. He told me that the police jury had a conservation fund, that the money had been there for years, doing nothing. Maybe $1,200. It was money from hunting licenses, the parish got a part of it.

"Johnny said to me, 'Cat, you're a game warden. You work for the state. Only a game warden can draw out this money. Maybe you can get yourself appointed game warden for the parish.

"So I went to Sheriff Thibodeaux and I said 'Mister Charlie, I'm a game warden, and if you give me the parish job I can draw this money. It's not doing nothing anyway'. So he give me the commission, at $35 a month. I guess I did that for two-three years, until the fund was used up."

His other job was serving as bailiff during federal court sessions.

"I got that job because I was friendly with George Montgomery, the United States marshal. My job was to mind the door, to keep people from crowding the courtroom too much." Federal court sessions would attract large numbers of people from the six parishes within the district because of the many persons charged with Prohibition violations.

This job also involved transporting federal prisoners to other jails in Louisiana and in other states.

"The government had contracts with jails in Shreveport, Marksville and Oberlin. And I went with the deputy marshal once or twice to drive prisoners to Portland, Oregon, and Seattle, Washington.

"I was friendly with old Judge Dawkins. When he would adjourn court here in Opelousas I would drive him to Alexandria and he'd catch a train to Monroe. There was no connections from here."

Meanwhile, Cat's involvement with L. Austin Fontenot Sr. had been firmly established. And along with it his committment to Huey Long.

Cat made his first bid for public office in 1931. Governor Huey Long was campaigning for the United States Senate; he needed men in key positions in hard-to-control St. Landry. "Mister Austin" deemed this the proper time for his protege to cut his political teeth: Cat announced for the office of Opelousas city marshal, running against his cousin, Albert Clary.

The Clarion-News of October 17, 1931, carried a front page announcement:

"D. J. (Cat) Doucet announced Monday that he would seek election as city marshal in the coming Democratic Primary. At present, Mr. Doucet is connected with the State Conservation Department as well as Federal Game Warden.

"While commonly called city marshal, the office is known as constable of part of the first ward, including the city of Opelousas.

"Mr. Doucet is widely known and connected with one of the

27

larger families of the parish."

In the issue of October 22, 1931, with the qualifying deadline passed, the newspaper listed the candidates for parish offices:

Sheriff: Charles Thibodeaux, incumbent; Ariel Fontenot. Garland Dejean.

Assessor: Rene C. Fontenot, incumbent; Alex Lafleur, Dan Pollingue.

City judge: A. L. Andrus, incumbent; Edward S. Burleigh, Dr. A. J. Perrault.

City marshal: Albert L. Clary, incumbent; D. J. (Cat) Doucet.

Henry Lastrapes, clerk of court, and Dr. B. A. Littell, coroner, were unopposed.

The city marshal candidate the voters of Ward One were asked to consider was nearing his 32nd birthday. He was a good looking young man, of commanding appearance and confident manner. A little under six feet tall, he was lean and broad-shouldered; he walked softly, but erect, with an almost military stance. He kept his brown hair neatly trimmed and combed, he dressed well and in good taste.

When he chose to use his considerable charm his brown eyes grew warm and confiding; he smiled easily and often. He had a whimsical sense of humor and knew well how to use his innate Cajun sense of the absurd to his own advantage. He was polite to women, deferential to his elders. Four decades later he would have been labeled "charismatic."

He was never considered a bad-tempered man, but was easily aroused to anger when he felt himself abused. "I liked to fight when I was young," he admits. "I got into lots of fights."

He was singularly outspoken and candid, and often showed a degree of naivete that dismayed his political cohorts. One of the stories about him, told by District Judge Lessley P. Gardiner, a former running mate, relates how, after prolonged deliberation by the faction to plan campaign strategy, Cat would go out and naively let every cat out of the bag.

"We learned to keep our mouths shut around Cat," said Judge Gardiner. "Unless it was something we wanted the whole parish to know about!"

The Doucet voice was perhaps Cat's most outstanding physical trait. Deep, articulate, resonant, he could project at will — at a political rally, on radio or television. This he had to learn on his own, by imitation, perhaps by listening to political speakers or by hearing and observing the old master, "Mister Austin," in the courtroom.

Once heard, that voice was not readily forgotten. "You didn't have to see him to know who was talking," said Ruth Robertson Fontenot. "Cat's voice was unique when he was making a speech. We could always recognize his voice."

And, notwithstanding his blithe disregard of the nuances of the English language, he had the gift of oratory.

The lead story in the Clarion-News of January 14, 1932, announced that the newspaper would broadcast the returns of the forthcoming election over loudspeakers. A leased wire would bring in the state returns; arrangements had been made to get parish returns from each precinct via long distance telephone. The public was invited to the election party, and the newspaper management promised to continue giving returns until the results were decisive.

Headlines after the election told the story: "Big Majority for O. K. Allen" and "Sheriff Thibodeaux Wins Over Two Opponents." The Long faction had swept the state, but the anti-Long forces were victorious in St. Landry.

The Opelousas city marshal kept his post and Cat was defeated. The official tabulation showed Albert Clary with 1,149 votes, while Ward One voters gave Cat 788. Cat's cousin Albert had a majority of 363 votes.

Sheriff Thibodeaux had soundly defeated his two opponents. Two other anti-Long incumbents, Rene Fontenot, assessor, and Kelly Andrus, city judge, had impressive majorities. The Long "complete the works" machine had hardly put a dent in the St. Landry fenders.

So St. Landry settled down for another four-year cease-fire, and Cat went back to his game warden job. The new United States senator, Huey Long, was busy with his "share the wealth" propa-

The Cat and St. Landry

ganda while continuing to rule the roost in Louisiana, and Franklin Delano Roosevelt became the 32nd president of the United States.

4

"We Took Three"

During the summer of 1935 the Louisiana political pot was at a full, rolling boil. Senator Huey Long, who had indeed given Louisiana school children free books, eliminated the poll tax, reduced auto license tags and improved roads, instigated legislation that lit the dynamite fuse in St. Landry.

This was the year that James Cagney headed the list of 12 best actors; when Claudette Colbert and Clark Gable won the Academy Award for "It Happened One Night' . . .

Newspaper editorials cautiously predicted the return of better times . . . rumblings of a war in Europe triggered cartoons and editorial comments to the effect that America had best stay out of the mess . . . the 18th Amendment had been repealed . . . Bruno Hauptman was being tried for the kidnapping and brutal murder of the Lindberg baby.

National concern was aroused when terriffic dust storms hit Oklahoma . . . Admiral Richard Byrd was back from his second expedition to the South Pole . . . the condition of banks in St. Landry Parish was reported " better" . . . .

Among the bills introduced in the Louisiana House that summer was one extending state control over parish school boards. School boards would no longer hire and fire teachers. Instead, names of all prospective teachers and the amounts of their salaries would be submitted to a state screening committee.

Another bill would regulate the conduct of elections. Instead of each candidate furnishing a list of names from which the parish board would draw names of election commissioners and clerks, all poll officials would be named by the state, or in effect, by Governor O. K. Allen, Huey's "yes man."

Both measures aroused strong sentiment in St. Landry. The Opelousas newspaper voiced protest, public meetings were called, official statements were made.

The hatchet fell quickly. The state law authorizing the governor, state treasurer and superintendent of education to supervise operations of parish school boards resulted in the immediate firing of 16 St. Landry Parish teachers, including two principals.

Banner headlines in the Clarion-News sounded the call to arms: "Fight School Politicalization!" The story told of public reaction to the action of the local school board, which had voted 6-3 to oust the 16 teachers, all known for their anti-Long affiliations.

This was the "screening" on the parish level, the paper said, engineered by the Long members of the school board. The list of "approved" teachers had still to be submitted to the state committee before any could be hired. The newspaper predicted that even more heads might fall. The ruling also affected janitors and transfer (bus) drivers.

The paper announced a mass meeting at the courthouse, devoted three full columns to a blow-by-blow account of the school board meeting. The front page story carried the names of the 16 teachers who had been fired "without cause."

On the back page was a listing of teachers recommended for jobs by the pro-Longs, also a list submitted by the parish superintendent of education.

The move was plainly an extension of the Long machine's power grab, and was understood as such by all. Anti-Long and pro-Long members of the school board were easily identified by the way they voted. One of the fired principals told the school board: "The only reason for such board action is politics, which can be laid at the door of Senator Huey P. Long."

The anti-Long forces went into action. The following week the Opelousas newspaper reported:

"Indignant citizens from all sections of St. Landry flay school board members here Thursday night at a mass meeting."

The Opelousas protest meeting was described as "one of the largest ever held in the courthouse." The second floor of the court building was said "packed to capacity, the crowd overflowing to the square below. Traffic was stopped for four blocks as loud speakers carried protest talks to eager listeners."

The Long faction called a mass meeting in Eunice, the second largest town in the parish, "to explain" the new ruling. The Opelousas newspaper reported: "The city hall, which will seat about 500, was not filled."

Nonetheless, almost equal time was given the Eunice meeting. L. Austin Fontenot Sr., who was always "good copy," was quoted at length; the names of non-Eunice residents attending the meeting were listed. The list included D. J. (Cat) Doucet, identified as "a candidate for office on the Long ticket in this parish."

The following week found the controversy partially resolved. The paper of September 8, 1935, reported that the St. Landry School Board's list of teachers had been approved by the state budget committee with no more teacher names dropped. Some of the fired teachers had been reinstated, and the list of teachers ousted had dropped from 16 to eight, plus several janitors and bus drivers.

Two other major issues, state control of poll officials and the re-districting of St. Landry, were not to come to a head in the parish until after the funeral of Senator Long, who died September 10, 1935, 30 hours after he was shot in the state capitol.

The Clarion-News of September 12, 1935 — the same issue that carried a lengthy, detailed article about the state funeral of Senator Long — informed the public of the motives behind the house bill that divided the 13th Judicial District:

"Realization of the extent to which reprisal politics would lead a man in his grasp for power and ability to punish his opponents was understood in St. Landry early Monday morning, when it was learned that the present special session of the legislature had passed a bill that divorced this parish from Evangeline, the two comprising the Thirteenth Judicial District.

"In this divorce bill, St. Landry would be linked with Lafayette, Acadia and Vermilion Parishes in the Fifteenth Judicial District. Evangeline Parish will be the sole political subdivision of the Thirteenth Judicial District.

"In making this move, Judge B. H. Pavy will become a secondary figure in the Fifteenth Judicial District, and District Attorney R. Lee Garland will become an assistant district attorney."

In a strongly-worded editorial, the newspaper editor labeled the bill "another step taken towards punishing men who have been politically opposed to the present powers that be," and called for repeal of the bill.

(Thirty-five years later, Cat Doucet summarized the matter thus: "There was the Pavy faction, and the Huey Long - Austin Fontenot faction. Judge Pavy, Lee Garland, Willie Dejean, all anti-Long. Huey changed the judicial district. He put St. Landry in with those other parishes, all together. That way Judge Pavy would have to run in four parishes to be judge, and so would Lee Garland. And that's how Huey got rid of them.")

The Kingfish was dead, of an assassin's bullet fired by Judge Pavy's son-in-law. But all of the seeds he had sown were not yet to be reaped by the whirlwind . . . .

At this time Cat was being readied as a first-time candidate for a major office in a parish known to be anti-Long. He had long been aligned with the Long faction, and it was to be assumed that he would go along with anything proposed by Long leaders. ("I always listened to Mister Austin").

But when a third state-level political controversy arose, the Cat stopped purring and showed his claws.

"Yep, me and Austin we had a serious difference. I told him I would get out the race — that I didn't want to win if the other side had no representation."

This was at the end of 1935, when the 1936 election campaign was running red hot. Tempers on both sides were short; serious issues were involved and more and more St. Landry citizens were being drawn into the conflict.

Cat claims that he and "Old Man Austin" almost came to a parting of the ways over the election bill.

This was one of the so-called "reform bills" (passed by the legislature at Huey's dictation during the special session) which abolished the system of drawing names of election officials (commissioners, clerks, watchers) from names submitted by candidates for office. Instead, the bill placed this function in the hands of a parish board, members of which were appointed by the governor.

The Clarion-News had a lot to say about the matter. The issue of October 3, 1935 carried a full report on the meeting of the State Central Committee in Baton Rouge, at which a resolution to give candidates equal representation had been denied:

"L. Austin Fontenot, prominent legal luminary of the Opelousas bar, delivered an ultimatum speech at the meeting of the State Central Committee . . . "

The paper did not so state, but the implication was that Mr. Austin's "ultimatum speech" had resulted in the 80 to 13 defeat of the resolution calling for equal representation.

The article continued:

" . . . in which he (Fontenot) is quoted as having said, following a heated debate, that the way to treat the opposition was 'to sit them down, stomp 'em down, and hold 'em down.' He is the St. Landry leader of former Senator Huey P. Long and present Governor O. K. Allen forces."

But the parish board refused to be "stomped down." The three members of the St. Landry Parish Board of Election Supervisors went on public record on October 17 as being in favor of both sides having representation at the polls. Individual statements to this effect were signed by Paul Fontenot, board chairman; Ernest McKinney and L. A. Gosselin.

Cat Doucet had not yet qualified as a candidate for sheriff. He had been identified in the paper as "a candidate," but no official announcement had appeared in the Opelousas newspaper.

All during the fall the front page of the Clarion-News carried stories of candidates announcing; each issue had dozens of paid political announcements (small, classified ad-type announcements; no display ads), but none carried the name of D. J. (Cat) Doucet.

A front page story of October 17 listed the names of candidates who had qualified. Still no Doucet for sheriff. Qualifying deadline was October 21, until midnight.

Finally, in the issue of October 24, Cat's name was on the published list of candidates who had qualified. The newspaper summed up the situation as follows:

"Sheriff Charles Thibodeaux, thrown in a three-candidate race, is against the state administration and as a result is facing a campaign for re-election against D. J. Doucet and Dudley J. Briley. Both Mr. Doucet and Mr. Briley have state administration connections."

The newspaper noted the doubling up of pro-Long candidates: "Contested races, in practically every instance, found one candidate representing anti-administration and two candidates making the race on a state administration ticket."

The controversy over the split-up of the 13th Judicial District ended up in the courts. The district court decision was, the Opelousas newspaper stated; "so involved that attorneys of Louisiana will be discussing the question of the issue for years to come."

There was other material of lively interest to newspaper readers. The paper reminded readers which of the candidates had gone along with the administration on "politicalization of the schools." Headlines and stories told of activities of the opposing factions, "the Long Machine" and the "Home Rule Ticket." Later, these titles were shortened to simply "The Machine" and "Home Rulers." The word machine had become synonymous with the state administration; "Home Rulers" included everybody opposed to "The Machine."

One report said that a congressional committee would investigate "charges of attempted irregularities in the impending election." Background of the expected irregularities and investigation was given:

"The investigating committee was appointed by the Lower House of Congress last summer before the death of Senator Long when charges were openly voiced that candidates opposing the state administration in Louisiana would have no chance of election with the state administration in full control of the election machinery.

"Since Senator Long's death, demand has been made on the state machine leaders for equal representation of election commissioners at the polls in January. Nothing has been done, so far, beyond a statement by Governor Allen that both sides would have representation. The law empowering the board of election supervisors (appointed by the governor) to select election commissioners is still in effect."

Meanwhile, a squabble had begun between the two parish newspapers: the anti-Long Clarion News of Opelousas, and the pro-Long New Era of Eunice. The controversy was to provide lively reading for St. Landry citizens for quite some time.

The newspaper editors blasted each other while castigating the political faction each was fighting. The Opelousas newspaper, for the Home Rulers, charged that the Eunice paper, which had previously been anti-Long, was now backing four candidates "who were instrumental in politicalizing the schools." The Opelousas paper called the Eunice publication "the Baton Rouge paper, published in Eunice."

The Opelousas paper continued its campaign for equal representation at the polls. Reporting on the December meeting of the police jury, the editor wrote:

"Like Banquo's ghost, the equality of candidates at the polls at the January primary came back to haunt the St. Landry Police Jury Tuesday and resulted in a nine-to-two vote favoring fair representation to both factions at the approaching balloting."

The victory, it would seem, had not been easy:

"Tuesday morning members of the police jury approved a resolution to give equal representation in poll commissioners after a similar resolution had been defeated twice Monday."

The "double harness" ticket also came under fire. The newspaper declared that magic slogan, "Share the Wealth," a "dead issue," and scorned L. Austin Fontenot's feeble defense of the doubling up of pro-administration candidates:

" . . . the administration mouthpiece in St. Landry attempted to defend the 'dual office holding class ticket' otherwise the 'double harness' ticket of both state and parish candidates, and the dead issue of 'Share the Wealth.'"

Cat Doucet and Dudley Briley were the administration candidates for sheriff.

"Having us both run, that was Mister Austin's idea," says Cat. "The way it was supposed to work, I vote for one, my wife votes for the other. But Old Man Austin was with me, one hundred per cent. We was just using Dudley, and he knew that. We wanted to beat old man Charlie Thibodeaux, see? Wanted to throw Charlie into a second race."

But "old man Charlie" wasn't going to be in the second race, or the first race either. Less than two months before the first primary, Sheriff Thibodeaux died. The 68-year-old sheriff, nearing the end of his fourth term of office, died in a Marlin, Texas hospital as a result of blood poisoning.

On the heels of this announcement, Simon Stelly, Sheriff Thibodeaux's chief deputy, qualified as a candidate for the office of sheriff.

The Democratic Executive Committee, after a special meeting, re-opened the time of qualification as prescribed under Louisiana law, and Stelly, chief deputy for six years, qualified for the race as an anti-administration candidate.

The law also provided that the coroner, at that time Dr. B. A. "Buster" Littell, an anti-Long, was to fill the unexpired term of the sheriff. Unless the governor saw fit to appoint someone else. And Governor O. K. Allen did see fit to do so; two weeks after Sheriff Thibodeaux's death he appointed one of his own men, John I. Beard.

The political machinery of St. Landry slowed down only momentarily after the death of Sheriff Thibodeaux.

The "equal rights" battle continued in full force. Other groups, such as the Opelousas and Washington American Legion posts, joined the police jury in adopting resolutions calling for equal representation for both factions at the polls in the forthcoming election.

The board of election supervisors declared that both political factions would have equal representation. The unanimous resolution provided that each side would have two commissioners and alternates at each poll, the fifth commissioner to be drawn from names submitted by both factions.

Three of the "machine" candidates objected. The newspaper reported:

"W. F. Brown, candidate for assessor, and D. J. Doucet and Dudley Briley, both for sheriff, took exception to the ruling and issued statements saying that such action by the election supervisors would prove unfair to them."

The three disclaimed that they were running on "the machine" ticket, but were running on the "Share the Wealth" platform. They claimed that if the commissioners were to be named by faction campaign managers that they would have no representation as individual candidates. Their statements were printed in full. Readers could readily recognize the high-flown Austin Fontenot phraseology.

"Of course Old Man Austin wrote those statements," said Cat. "I couldn't of wrote them, and Dudley didn't have as much education as me."

The action of the election board didn't please Mister Austin. Nor did it please Governor O. K. Allen. He removed the names of two members from the St. Landry board and appointed two others in their stead.

"That was Austin behind that," says Cat. "He didn't want the opposition to have any representation at all. We had quite an argument about it."

Cat said he told Austin that he didn't want to be elected unless his opponents had representation at the polls.

"You see, that was before we had voting machines. The commissioners could do what they wanted. And if I got elected I didn't want it to be that way.

"That's when I told Austin I'd get out the race unless the other side had representation.

"And that's when we give them two and we took three."

The showdown came at the meeting of the St. Landry Parish Board of Election Supervisors. The meeting moved along quietly, the paper stated, "with a large number of prominent citizens from every section of the parish present." The Home Rule ticket was permitted to submit the names of two commissioners for each poll, and the opposing faction "took three."

(Cat's defiance of his political mentor's wishes at this time is discounted by some who were closely involved in the Fontenot-Doucet alliance: "Cat Doucet never opposed anything proposed by Austin Fontenot").

Came election day and Simon Stelly, as was expected, was high man in the Democratic primary with 4,934 votes. Cat was right behind with 3,639, and the other member of the "double harness" team, Dudley Briley, received 2,933. Old Man Austin's strategy had worked; Stelly was thrown into a run-off with Cat.

The Cat and St. Landry

Deaths of three other political figures were to further complicate the campaign of 1936. After Sheriff Thibodeaux's death, the Home Rulers lost another strong contender, Dr. G. P. Garland of Eunice, candidate for the state senate. Dr. Garland died of pneumonia, said to have been contracted while he stood in the rain during a political rally. His death came on December 14, 1935, five weeks before the first primary.

In the first primary, Lennie Savoy of Eunice, administration candidate for clerk of court, had been defeated by Henry Lastrapes, the incumbent. Mr. Lastrapes had been the only Home Rule candidate to achieve a decisive victory.

The incumbent assessor, Rene Fontenot, was thrown into a second race with W. F. Brown, the administration candidate. But before the second primary death claimed both Fontenot and Brown, leaving no candidates in the field. Two new candidates entered the race: Lennie Savoy, the defeated administration candidate for clerk of court, and Ariel Fontenot, a Home Ruler.

Returns of the second primary of March 3, 1936, showed Doucet, 7,050 votes; Stelly, 4,163.

Cat Doucet was the new sheriff of St. Landry Parish. He had won a decisive victory, but not exactly "by a landscape," the classic prediction attributed to him in later campaigns.

Cat carried 27 of the 31 precincts. Stelly led in four precincts: Bristol, Cankton, Notleyville and Plaquemine Point.

All of the administration candidates were victorious. Their leader, L. Austin Fontenot Sr., issued a statement, the purpose of which, the paper said, "was to bring harmony between opposing forces:"

"The long-drawn out political battle which was started in this parish in August, 1935, is over, and I am glad; the outcome was a smashing and glorious victory for our side, and this makes me gladder."

Some 35 years afterwards former sheriff Doucet summed up his early years in politics thus:

"Four years after Albert Clary beat me for city marshal, I ran against Charlie Thibodeaux, sheriff for 16 years. Mr. Charlie was getting old, so I thought I had a chance to get elected. And he died during his campaign, poor man, he died at Marlin, Texas. That's when his chief deputy, Simon Stelly, jumped in there and ran in his place. Mr. Stelly didn't have time to campaign. It was too close to election."

After the tumult of the 1936 elections the parish settled down to more mundane affairs, and the Cat sneaked into the courthouse before time. Several months before he took his oath of office, the sheriff-elect was appointed a deputy by Sheriff Beard.

His deputy activities were noted in the local press. One story reported that Deputy Doucet, with two other deputies, had removed an alleged slayer to a Baton Rouge jail, "fearing mob lynching." Another dealt with an incident in which Cat, with three other lawmen, apprehended a bad check artist "in a chase which ended up in New Orleans." Another concerned Deputy Cat helping the sheriff arrest a robbery suspect in Palmetto.

Today, Cat remembers only the Palmetto robbery.

"That was at Allen Budden's store," he said. "They broke in there two-three times in two weeks and stole cigarettes.

"I'll tell you how they did that. The railroad passes right across the street from the store. When the train would pass, around midnight, it would make lots of noise. That's when they would break a window and jump in there."

The Clarion-News of April 30, 1936, devoted a paragraph to Cat's forthcoming inauguration, and added a brief review of the succession of St. Landry sheriffs:

"Sheriff-elect D. J. Doucet, now a deputy, will be one of the first to officially take office. Doucet's entry into office is expected to follow shortly the inauguration of Governor-designate Richard Leche on May 12.

"It has now been 16 years since the St. Landry electorate has placed a new man in that office. The late Sheriff Charles Thibodeaux, who was succeeded a few months ago by J. I. Beard, was elected in 1920.

"Previous terms were held by Darius Fontenot, and before that, M. L. Swords, who served four successive terms since 1900. Before that, W. F. Frazee and H. H. Deshotels."

Records of land sales in the St. Landry Parish sheriff's office, dating back to 1810, seven years after the Louisiana Purchase, confirm Cat's claim that he was sheriff longer than anyone else in the history of the parish.

In 1810, J. Cornelius Voorhies signed the record book as "sheriff of the fifth superior court district of the territory of Orleans." After him came Sam E. McIntire, then Theophilus Collins, the first to sign himself "sheriff of St. Landry Parish."

From that time (1822) until the Civil War sheriffs were Benjamin L. Haw, George Jackson, Lewis Andrus, James Morgan, John I. Taylor, Harrison Rogers, P. L Petit, Baptiste David and Louis V. Chachere.

Sheriff Chachere took office in 1856 and was still sheriff in 1862. No land sales were recorded from that year until 1865, when the book was signed by Sheriff J. J. Beauchamp.

James G. Hayes was sheriff in 1866, and his successors were T. S. Fontenot, James M. Thompson, Egbert O. Hayes and C. C. Duson.

During this 160-year period long-term sheriffs were C. C. Duson, 14 years; M. L. Swords and Charles Thibodeaux, each 16 years; D. J. "Cat" Doucet, 20 years.

Cat Doucet was 36 years old when he was sworn in as sheriff of St. Landry. He was no longer an amateur in the field; he knew he had been elected in the wake of the wave of pro-Long sentiment that had swept the state after the assassination of Huey.

And like Huey, Cat was either much liked or much disliked; it was not possible for constituents to remain indifferent. One was either for him, or against him.

From the start he exhibited the characteristics that earned for him the label "born politician." Once an election was over, he put personal grudges aside.

"I never stopped talking to nobody," he said. "You can't win like that."

Also in those early years stories about Cat began to be circulated; the type of stories that caused some to dismiss him as an ignorant clown. No doubt some of these stories were true, but certainly many were manufactured and attributed to him. He was "a natural;" exactly the type of public figure that invited such inventions.

For instance, the story about the campaign funds, which goes as follows:

Cat and his ticket mates were discussing who was to have charge of the campaign money. Someone suggested putting it in the bank in a certain fellow's name, another said "how about putting it in escrow?"

To which Cat answered:

"That's all right with me, but I don't know that fellow S. Crow. Better give me his address and phone number."

The first time Cat made the paper after he was sworn in was on June 4, 1936. A two-column picture, a rare thing in those days, of mail order cuts, was captioned: "Miss Irene 'Two-Gun' Shute." The cutline said that Sheriff Doucet had appointed Miss Shute a St. Landry deputy, and that the new lady deputy had laughingly described herself as "Two-Gun Irene."

Irene Shute was one of the most respected and well-liked residents of Opelousas. The sister of a prominent physician, member of a pioneer family, the appointment of this genteel lady was nothing less than political genius. (No precedent was set; Sheriff Thibodeaux had named the first lady deputy in the parish, Miss Velma Pressburg).

"It was my idea, not Austin's, to make Miss Irene a deputy," Cat said. "That was because when them poor people would come to me when they had sickness, I'd send them to Shute's Drug Store and Miss Irene would only charge me half, maybe less, to get their medicine.

"And she had some duties. It wasn't wasting the taxpayers' money. Lots of times we had women prisoners and we'd call Miss Irene to search 'em.

"When Miss Irene died she left a paper. On it were the names of the people she wanted for her pallbearers. And my name was on that paper, the first one. I'm real proud of that. She was one of the best people I ever knew."

In November of that year St. Landry was again "divorced," this time from the 15th Judicial District where it had been placed with Acadia, Lafayette and Vermilion in the punitive action instigated by Huey to oust Judge Pavy and Lee Garland. The parish was placed in a separate judicial district designated as the 27th.

Governor Richard Leche announced the appointment of a new district judge, Isom J. Guillory of Eunice, and a new district attorney, L. Austin Fontenot, both to take office on Jan. 1, 1937.

This brought the new sheriff and his long-time friend and advisor into an even closer relationship.

The year 1936 and most of 1937 passed without major incident in the sheriff's department. Sheriff Doucet's name was mentioned in the press only in connection with local sports activities.

The sheriff was one of several leaders who conducted a fund drive to bring a district football game to Opelousas. The undefeated Opelousas High School Tigers were to meet the strong Amite Warriors, also undefeated, and in order to get the game played on the home field it was necessary to raise $500. The drive was successful.

The Tigers won the game, 7-0, "despite freezing temperatures" the paper said, and some 1,500 football fans attended. The next district play-off was against the Vinton High eleven, and again the local fans, including the sheriff, backed the drive for $750 to get the game played in Opelousas.

The required amount was raised in a short canvass of the business district, plus a $100 donation from the Chamber of Commerce and another $100 given by the "Courthouse — City Hall Fund."

The game ended in a 7-7 tie, but Opelousas High's 11 first downs matched the home team against Minden for the state championship title. Again the local leaders staged a fund drive to get the game for Opelousas — the third such in three weeks. The amount of money needed was not mentioned in the newspaper.

The drive was again successful, Opelousas got the game, but the home team suffered its first defeat, after 15 straight wins. The Minden team outscored the Tigers 34-6 and won the state title. The newspaper, loyal to the end, carried this headine after the game:

"Opelousas High Is Victorious in Minden Win." A subhead explained the cryptic heading:

"Fighting Opelousas Team Outscored but Gallant Stand Draws Favorable Comment from Fans." Another consolation prize was that Bud Ducharme, Tiger captain, had been placed in the second all-star high school team at tackle by Harry Martinez, New Orleans States' sports writer.

"Yeh, I remember all that," said Cat. "Three times we did that. But our boys lost the championship. That money from the courthouse and city hall, that must have been the slot machine fund.

"And one time me and Austin and Henry Larcade, we took the school children, those that wanted to go, to the race track in New Orleans. We got a bunch of busses. It was Opelousas Day at the tracks."

Thus a year and a half went by, almost uneventfully. Never again was Cat Doucet, as sheriff, to experience such a lengthy time of tranquility.

45

5

The Last Hanging

Elgie Stephens was the son of a Negro tenant farmer on Dubuisson Plantation in the northern sector of the parish. He grew up on the plantation and worked in the cotton fields with his parents. When he was 22, Elgie married Rubilene Nichols, described as a "good looking" young woman.

Stephens was jealous of his wife. They quarreled often, and she left him several times.

A share cropper like his father, Elgie had little money until he sold his cotton each fall. In October of 1937, the crop sold, he gave Rubilene $16, with which to buy herself some clothes.

Asked how she had spent the money, Rubilene told Elgie she had spent $10 on clothes and used the remaining $6 to repay a debt she owed her grandmother. Elgie didn't believe this; he believed his wife had used the $6 to buy a train ticket to Houston — that she planned to leave him again.

They quarreled; the argument became violent. Elgie knocked his wife down several times, finally left her lying unconscious on the floor. Afterwards, Rubilene packed her belongings and went to her father's house.

Elgie went to the plantation commissary and bought a bottle of whiskey. He brooded as he drank. In a jealous rage, his anger fed by alcohol, he got a shotgun and went to his father-in-law's house. He fired the gun through a partially opened window shutter. The charge blew off the back of Rubilene's head.

The murder at Dubuisson Plantation was virtually overshadowed, as far as public sentiment was concerned, by another murder which had taken place several days before at the opposite end of the parish. Lester Senegal, a young Negro yard man, had damaged his employer's car in a minor accident. Without the car owner's knowledge, he had the car repaired. The repair bill, totaling $5.90, was sent to the owner, and the law was sent after Senegal.

When Gabriel Burleigh, Sunset town marshal, came to arrest

Senegal, the Negro shot and fatally wounded the peace officer. Burleigh died instantly; Senegal fled into a nearby field and escaped.

It is a coincidence that a small sum of money was the spark that triggered both murders. It is significant that both cases, in totally different ways, were to influence the future of the 38-year-old sheriff, who had been in office less than 18 months.

Elgie Stephens was arrested, charged with murder, and incarcerated in the parish jail. A month later, on November 10, 1937, Stephens was indicted for the murder of his wife by the St. Landry Parish Grand Jury. The court-appointed attorney for the defense was J. Y. Fontenot, son of the district attorney, L. Austin Fontenot Sr.

The district attorney's charge, as returned by the grand jury, read as follows: "That one Elgie Stephens, at the parish of St. Landry, on or about October 10, 1937, feloniously, wilfully, unlawfully, and of his malice and aforethought, did kill and murder one Rubilene Nichols Stephen."

Stephens was tried twice, the first time on November 22, 1937, 12 days after his indictment. The verdict of the all-white jury was "guilty as charged." Motion for a new trial was granted by District Judge Isom J. Guillory, and the second trial was held in June of 1938. The second jury, also all-white, returned the same verdict. Both verdicts were unanimous. Sentence was pronounced: death by hanging.

Attorneys for the defense, J. Y. Fontenot and E. G. Burlegih (also court-appointed), filed motion for a third trial. On October 31, 1938, the Louisiana Supreme Court, with Justice John B. Fournet as the organ of the court, affirmed the conviction and sentence of the accused.

During the months of his imprisonment Elgie Stephens made friends in the courthouse. The young Negro was dark, of medium height, stockily built, and muscular from field work and hoisting cotton bales at the plantation gin. But he was in no way menacing in appearance. He had an easy smile and friendly manner, and was a docile prisoner. Until the murder he had not been involved in trouble of any sort. He was not a criminal type; his had been a crime of passion. He was termed "a good nigger" by his cell mates.

Not the least among his new-found friends was the sheriff himself.

Governor Richard Leche signed the death warrant January 21, 1939, and the document was read to Stephens by Sheriff Doucet on the morning of January 27. The convicted man listened to the sheriff without showing any emotion, "maintaining the same calm that had been characteristic of him since he had been arrested 18 months before," the newspaper reported. Stephens was placed in solitary confinement.

After the death warrant was read, Stephens' attorneys made a last attempt to save his life. They circulated a petition — which was signed by the sheriff, a number of other parish officials and members of the two petit juries who had served on the case — asking that the death sentence be changed to life imprisonment. A special hearing was set for February 11, six days before the execution date.

From the beginning District Attorney Fontenot had pushed for the death penalty. At the time the petition was being circulated and the special hearing set, the district attorney was away, on some mission outside the state. When he returned and learned what was going on, he ordered those public officials who had signed the petition to remove their names from the document. Most of them, including the sheriff, obeyed.

Reporting on the hearing in New Orleans, the Opelousas newspaper stated "it was father against son." The district attorney brought with him to the hearing key witnesses in the case, and "vigorously presented the evidence of two convictions and the details of the shooting." He insisted that the letter and spirit of the law be carried out.

Serving on the pardon board were Judge Isom Guillory, who had sat on the bench for the two trials; Lt. Gov. Earl Long and a representative from the attorney general's office. Judge Guillory, it was reported, had sent in his recommendation for commutation of sentence in writing.

The plea for clemency was turned down.

Informed that only the remote chance of executive clemency on the part of Governor Leche could save him, Elgie Stephens made two requests: that he be allowed to talk to his father and mother before he was executed, and secondly, for permission to go into the jail dining room and eat with the other prisoners. Sheriff Doucet told him arrangements would be made for his parents to visit, also granted his request to eat with the other prisoners instead of in solitary confinement. But Elgie took only a cup of coffee, then returned to his cell.

District Attorney Fontenot, questioned by a reporter, gave the following statement:

"Our kind hearted district judge was very anxious that this Negro not be hung. Of course, everyone is entitled to his or her opinion of the facts.

"After having been with the case since the morning of October 11, 1937, I am of the opinion that he should be hung. Personally, I could see no extenuating circumstances."

Besides Judge Guillory, "many officials" approved the commutation of sentence for the accused, the newspaper story said. Apparently in justification of his stand in the matter, the district attorney continued with a summary of the crime:

"From the outside in the dark with a shotgun, he (Stephens) opened a crack in the window and aimed the gun to the back of his wife's head while she was sitting on the sofa in the light with her back to the window. There is no doubt about this, as the defendant, Elgie Stephens, openly admitted this to Deputy Sheriff Tom Ware and to Coroner Dr. S. E. Graham.

"Stephens' only excuse was that he had given his wife some money to buy clothes with and that she used a part of it to pay a debt which she honestly owed.

"It seems that her grandmother had loaned her $7 and that from the money given her by her husband to buy clothes for herself, she turned over $6 to her grandmother on the debt of $7.

"Of course, if in the heat of argument over the $6 he had shot his wife, it possibly could have been said that it was manslaughter instead of murder. However, the cold and unquestioned facts are that, in the presence of his own mother, he beat his wife

49

up for the $6 about noon on the day of the killing and actually struck his own mother, either purposely or accidentally when she tried to stop him from beating his wife. When he had her unconscious on the floor, he left and his wife, with the assistance of his mother, packed her little belongings and went to the home of her father, Esau Nichols, for protection and it was at Esau's house that she was killed.

"Some people don't believe in capital punishment. Our lawmakers have made capital punishment the law of this state. Until the law is changed, public officials who are sworn to uphold the law must see that the law is carried out or we will be changing the law ourselves when the only power to change the law is in the state legislature."

The district attorney knew the law. The law said Elgie Stephens must die by hanging. And it was Sheriff Doucet's duty to get the job done.

The hanging was to be a first for the young sheriff, although he had assisted Sheriff Thibodeaux with an execution some four years before, during his brief term as special deputy and game warden. The man hanged was a Negro by the name of Thomas, who had been convicted of the murder of T. T. deValcourt, a Sunset peace officer.

The day before the execution, the gruesome preparations had been completed by the sheriff. The rope had been properly stretched with a heavy sack of sand. The black cap, to be fitted over the condemned man's head just before the trap was sprung, had been made and was on hand. The coffin had been ordered.

Newspaper readers were given a preview of things to come:

"The death trap is located on the top floor of the jail. It is a small trap door in the floor with a mechanism, controlled by a handle, that permits it to drop down when the lever is pulled. First the black cap is placed over a condemned man's head, then the noose is fitted around his neck.

"With the noose around the neck and the cap over the head, the condemned man is guided to the trap. The lever is pulled and the body plunges down about five or six feet, depending on the rope. The knot on the side of the neck breaks the spinal cord

50

between the shoulders and the head.

"After the body has dropped through the trap, the coroner uses a stethoscope to listen to the lessening murmurs of the heart and finally declares the man dead. Usually the death pronouncement comes between eight and 12 minutes after the final 'go' is pulled on the lever."

Crowds milled around the courthouse square the day of the execution. What went on during the final 37 minutes of Elgie Stephens' life was recorded by an eye-witness, James Bourdier, Opelousas Herald reporter:

"There are more than 1,000 morbidly curious persons blocking Market Street at the entrance of the St. Landry Parish jail Friday morning as I elbow my way through to gain entrance to the bastile where Elgie Stephens, a little later, is to pay with his life his debt to society for the murder of his wife.

"On the top step to the entrance to the jail, I paused to get a full view of that crowd. I looked first to the right and as far as my eyes could see, I could see faces seemingly staring at me and to the left — I saw the other portion with practically the same expressions. Perhaps some wondered just what I would see when I entered that chamber of death.

"As I studied these facial expressions, I saw pity, envy, fear; and on some, satisfaction that they were standing without these walls and would not witness this ordeal.

"We had all become well acquainted with Elgie Stephens, or Steve as he was familiarly known by everyone at the jail. This was the first time I had been called upon to witness an execution and I keenly felt the discomfiture of the situation. Deputy Sheriff Leon Myers met me just past the front door. We shook hands and later he asked me to go up and talk to Steve.

"It's 11:30 now, as Mr. Myers swings the huge door that allows one to enter the cell block proper. Deputy Myers locks the door behind us, and, through instinct, I count the steps as we climb to Steve's cell.

"Preacher D. D. Jenkins of the Baptist Church of Dubuisson, Steve's church, is standing at the door of Steve's cell, praying.

"When Steve saw me, the praying stopped, even though I protested.

"'Glad to see you, Boss,' Steve greets me.

"We shook hands.

"Before I had a chance to say anything, Steve says: 'I'm prepared to go. I have made peace with my Lord. I want to thank you gentlemen for all the favors you have done while I have been here.'

"We talked for several minutes, Steve's voice never faltering. He had prepared himself and later I saw with my own eyes the extent to which he had really prepared himself.

"His mother and father were there. His father, Henry Stephens, told me Steve was a good boy, but the jailers, Deputies 'Black' Deville and Leon Myers, had told me that before.

"Henry Stephens, the father, showed plainly the strain of the past few days. He follows Preacher Jenkins about the cell and seemed to find a certain comfort in what the preacher was saying to him.

"Steve called for bacon and two fried eggs for breakfast. He seemed to enjoy the meal, the deputies told me. But he refused the noon meal.

"I bid Steve goodby.

"It's high noon, now.

"That's the starting hour for the execution as set by Governor Richard W. Leche.

"I'm in the dining room of the jail when Sheriff Doucet enters. I follow after the deputies up the stairway which leads to Steve's cell.

"We paused at the second stairway landing. An officer speaks to another prisoner but I can't hear what they're saying.

"At Steve's cell, Sheriff Doucet enters. Steve told the sheriff beforehand that he wanted to say a few words 'publicly.'

"Down the steps to the front door again. Steve shows no emotion, no fear of his impending fate. He talks. He speaks clearly, his voice firm. He thanks the parish officials for the kindness shown him during his incarceration in the parish prison.

"'I'm ready to go. I have made peace with my Lord. I know that everyone here has done all they can to save my life.' Steve

52

said more than that but he seemed to be repeating his former statement.

"There's a strange expression upon the faces of that same crowd. What could they see? What could they hear? I repeatedly ask myself this question.

"Steve leads the way, flanked closely by Sheriff Doucet, Deputy Sheriff Eaise Bibbs, Deputy Sheriff 'Black' Deville, Deputy Sheriff Leon Myers and Deputy Sheriff Tom Ware, and others. We arrive at the entrance to the cell blocks.

"Deputy Sheriff Leon Myers unlocks the heavy steel door.

"Steve enters first, and just past the door he stops, and here's what he said:

"'Mr. Chank,' as Deputy Myers is sometimes called, 'I know that I'm just a Negro, but I want you to shake hands with me before I go.'

"There's a taut expression on Myers' face. He looks directly into Steve's eyes, and says: 'Sure Steve, goodby.' Steve shakes hands with Deputy Myers.

"We walk the stairway, climbing, always to that chamber of death. We, to witness the execution — and Steve to keep his appointment with death.

"Finally, we arrive at the 'Last Mile,' those last 11 steps. Steve walks firmly with Sheriff Doucet at his side. At the top of the last flight, I watch the expression on Steve's face but there is none. He is the same as he was a week ago — ready to go.

"Steve is very particular as he steps on the death trap. The trap is made in two sections. It opens in the middle when the trap is sprung. When the double doors part, it drops its human burden into space, halting with a sudden jerk when the end of the rope is reached.

"The condemned man looks down at his feet, places one foot on either side of the dividing line — one foot on each of the swinging doors.

"'Don't you want to take my shoes off Sheriff?' Steve asks. Sheriff Doucet told him it was not necessary, that they would be removed before he was placed in the coffin.

"'Let's leave them on, Steve,' Deputy Sheriff Black Deville said.

53

'You are wearing white socks and they may get dirty.'

"There is a deathly silence prevailing in this tower of death as the moments close in on Elgie Stephens. The silence is tense, the air of the small room is hard to breathe. I look around at the faces of the men about me. They're pale, drawn faces, most of them.

"'Steve, do you want anything?' It's Sheriff Doucet talking to his prisoner now. 'We want to give you your last request.'

"'Mr. Doucet, I'd like to have the preacher pray over me.'

"Preacher Jenkins steps forward and onto the trap that is later to send Elgie Stephens to his doom.

"It's 12:12 p.m. when Stephens adjusts himself on the doors of death.

"Preacher Jenkins begins his prayer. There's a sudden rustle among the little crowd of men who had come to witness the execution. I looked around and hats were being lifted off and heads bowed.

"It's 12:26 now. The prayers for Elgie Stephens have been completed. Preacher Jenkins and several spirtual advisors step aside and off the trap.

"Sheriff Doucet reaches into his right hand coat pocket and withdraws a black silk hood. He lifts his arms and places the hood over Stephens' head.

"A half minute later Sheriff Doucet has the hood in place. Deputy Sheriff Leon Myers has the rope in his hands. The hangman's knot has eight loops in it. I count them as I stand near Myers.

"Deputy Myers walks toward the condemned man, but Sheriff Doucet takes the rope from Myers and adjusts its loop over Stephens' head, draws it taut around his neck.

"It's 12:27 but only 15 minutes since he had entered the room of death, seemingly an eternity.

"Are you ready Steve? Goodby." It's Sheriff Doucet talking again, but Steve does not reply. The sheriff jerks the black iron lever near the south wall of the room. The doors open suddenly. It's 12:27½ p.m.

"There's a sickening thud. A weight had dropped. Small pieces of white plaster from the ceiling fall on the coats of several witnesses.

"Down below a man was dying at the end of a rope. The jaws of the trap had sprung back, locked, and out of the way — had performed their duty.

"Dr. S. E. Graham, St. Landry Parish coroner, steps up to the prostrate body, unbuttons a shirt button, inserts his stethoscope and, with watch in hand, listens to the last fleeting heartbeats.

"I look at my watch again. Its hands denote 12:38½ p.m. 'I pronounce this man dead.' That's Coroner Graham speaking. He made the statement to Sheriff D. J. Doucet.

"At 12:40, Sheriff Doucet was handed a large pocket knife and reaching high above his head, he severed the rope about a foot above Stephens' head, releasing the body.

"Elgie Stephens had paid the supreme price for the murder of his wife."

Official witnesses to the execution were Howard Strother and Murphy Guillory, Eunice; John Lafleur, Grand Prairie; Hypolite Ryder and Gantt Nicholson, Washington; Vincent Savoy, Opelousas.

Afterwards, Sheriff Doucet issued this statement:

"It was a very distasteful and disagreeable task, of course, but it was in the line of my duty and had to be done just as my other official duties are performed. The legislature has provided that death is the penalty for murder, and has provided that the sheriff is the official who must execute such a sentence, so I simply performed one of the duties for which the people elected me.

"Like the judge said in his public statement, I feel that everybody concerned performed their duties as they saw them. The district attorney, the jury, the attorneys appointed by the court, the governor, the Board of Pardons and all others concerned with the case simply performed their various duties in the matter. All that I hope is that in the future, no Negro, nor white person for that matter, will ever again commit a crime in St. Landry Parish which will require us to do again that which all of us were required to do under our oaths of office."

The sheriff's expressed hope was not to be. There were to be other death penalties exacted for crimes committed. But no more hangings.

Elgie Stephens was the last man to be hanged in St. Landry Parish.

Thirty two years have gone by since Cat Doucet hung Elgie Stephens.

"I used to didn't like to talk about it," he says. "But I'll never forget that.

"I had come to like the boy. I didn't want him to hang. He stayed right there in the jail for going on two years. We were friends. I called him Steve.

"Old Man Austin wrote that statement, more for himself than for me. He wanted the death penalty. I don't know why. He said it was his duty as prosecuting attorney.

"When he came back that time — he had gone to Kentucky — and found out about the petition, he hit the ceiling. He raised hell. He said we had to take our names off. I took mine off, Henry Larcade did too, but Lennie, he refused. I don't remember about the others, but I guess they listened to Austin. He was a strong character.

"You see, John Fournet, he was on the supreme court and he was friends with the Longs. And Earl — he was on the pardon board. And everybody knew that Dick Leche wouldn't buck Austin either."

Cat admits that he tried to get out of the role of executioner.

"I went and talked to the priest. He said it was all right, that I shouldn't get out, that it was my duty.

"Then I talked to Steve. I told him I could get a hired executioner. But he said, 'Sheriff, I want you to do it.'

"So I did. I promised him I would."

Another person involved with the hanging was Rev. A. W. Rosette, present pastor of Greater Mt. Calvary Baptist Church of Opelousas. Rev. Rosette, one of Stephens' spiritual advisors, was one of the Negro ministers at the hanging.

"I spent that last night with Elgie in the death cell," Rev. Rosette relates. "We talked and prayed the whole night."

Elgie imagined that he was hearing strange noises, Rev. Rosette said. He told the preacher that he could hear noises that sounded like chairs being overturned in the jail, and that he couldn't pray.

"I said, Elgie don't worry. You're dead already. You've confessed your crime to me. Tomorrow when the sheriff cuts that rope, I'll be right there to catch your body, and the Lord will have already snatched your soul. You didn't hear any noises. That was the devil trying to get your soul back. The devil doesn't want you to be a Christian.

"He was ready to die, as ready as anyone I've ever seen. He told me, 'my wife will never be able to leave me again. I loved her, and now we'll be together always."

The aging preacher was a young man then, but what he witnessed that day comes across with the clarity of day before yesterday.

"Mr. Cat didn't want to hang Elgie. He was pale as a sheet. We all knew he had been good to the boy, and we remembered.

"It took Elgie a long time to die. To those of us who watched it seemed a very long time. His body didn't spin, he just hung there, not moving. His neck didn't break, he strangled to death. I think maybe it was because the heel of one of his shoes caught on the edge of the trapdoor, because the noose slipped from under his ear to right under his chin."

The general sentiment among the black people of the community was that justice had been done, Rev. Rosette affirmed. Stephens had killed his wife, therefore must pay with his own life.

"Something else I remember very well," the preacher continued. "I wore my Prince Albert coat. It had cost me $100. When the sheriff cut down the body I was there to catch it just like I said I would. Elgie's nose began to bleed, and the blood got all over my Prince Albert coat. The stains wouldn't come out and I couldn't use it any more."

6

The Editors' Hassle

Big news in Opelousas in late June of 1939 was the forthcoming dedication of the new municipal swimming pool and city park. Elaborate plans were in the making for the event, set for July 4. Lt. Governor Earl K. Long, candidate for governor in the 1940 election was invited to be the main speaker. Also invited was Governor Richard Leche.

Earl Long accepted the invitation on June 19; two days later Governor Leche announced his intention to resign his office for reasons of ill health. This move automatically put Earl in the governor's chair.

Immediately, plans for the new governor's visit to Opelousas were expanded. Earl announced that he would donate five beeves for a free barbecue, to which everybody in the parish was invited. Some 12,000 persons were expected to attend the giant rally and barbecue.

The new $75,000 municipal pool and park — the first in the parish — were all but submerged in all the hoop-la for luring a crowd to hear what Uncle Earl had to say.

And before dedication day arrived, Uncle Earl found that he had plenty to say.

In Baton Rouge and around the state rumors of wrongdoing were flying faster than the "dee-ducts," and the "double dippers" were beginning to get ulcer symptoms. Greedy fingers dipping in the till had jammed the mechanism of the most powerful political machine in the south. The administration had no "repairmen" expert enough to keep the complex machinery from a complete power failure. The sound and acrid smell of popping fuses permeated the entire nation . . .

In Opelousas that July 4 to help dedicate the pool and park (but mainly to advance his candidacy for governor) Governor-by-default Earl Long disclaimed any part of the plundering of the state's coffers. He promised to help catch the culprits and pledged a clean sweep of the type of state officials who used "gold fixtures in their bathrooms" etcetera, etcetera.

In the months of investigation which followed, Earl Long did emerge from the mire without even any "ring-around-the-collar" on his white shirt. But before he could brush away the dust that had rubbed off on him, the Louisiana electorate had placed a reform candidate, Sam Jones, in the gubernatorial driver's seat.

For a long time to come everyone and everything connected with the Long regime were to be highly suspect . . .

During the last half of 1939 headlines and stories in the Opelousas Herald continued to inform the public of new developments in the Louisiana scandals. Federal grand juries were indicting persons in high places for bilking the state; taxpayers were aghast at the extent of the pilfering.

The flushing out of the miscreants spread to all sections of the state. In St. Landry, the formation of "The Voluntary Guardians of Clean Government" was announced, the purpose of which was "to clean up by striking hard and straight from the shoulder all graft that exists among public officials within our great state." The names of 15 charter members were listed.

Other newspaper stories told of what was going on elsewhere in the nation: Henry Ford, celebrating his 76th birthday, was said to be "most emphatic in asserting that no major conflict lies ahead," despite recurring threats of hostilities in Europe; a young housewife in Arkansas was fined $50 for wearing shorts on the street, and the jitterbug was the newest dance craze.

By mid-August the reform group had a new title, "The Guardians of Good Government." Membership had increased from the original 15 charter members to a total of 74; the group was commonly known as the "GeeGees."

The GeeGees called a mass meeting. There was talk of a possible riot and the chairman of the group asked the FBI for protection.

The GeeGees wanted some questions answered. The questions, made public through distribution of printed circulars, had to do with the operation of gambling devices in the parish, and about dual office holding and other "double dipping" practices in parish

59

affairs.

The newspaper editor wanted no part of it. A front page editorial in 10-point type across two columns the full length of front page let readers know that the paper was in no way a part of the witch hunt:

"Clean government is one thing and a political campaign is another . . . the campaign has its inception in the exposure of state graft and corruption . . . the Opelousas Herald is going to come in for a lot of criticism, mainly because it refuses to be used as a political football.

" . . . accusations and/or insinuations against a man's character need not necessarily be true . . . there appeared a circular on the streets of Opelousas . . . there were some accusations and/or insinuations in the circular that don't belong in a newspaper's columns but in court . . . when a true bill is returned by a grand jury, that is the time to start a newspaper story . . . "

The same issue of the paper reported that District Attorney Fontenot had advised Sheriff Doucet in a letter that complaints had been received concerning operations of slot machines in St. Landry, and that the Sheriff was to proceed with raids against all slot machine operators.

The district attorney was quoted as follows:

"Whether the purpose of the demand for enforcement be political or whether it be an attempt to make a goat does not deserve consideration from the officials of the law."

In the letter to the sheriff, which was printed verbatim in the paper, the district attorney "respectfully suggested" that the sheriff immediately notify all the mayors, and all constables, and chiefs of police to take steps to stop the operation of slot machines in their neighborhoods.

"Mister Austin's" power as faction leader was unquestioned. Even his foes agreed that he was a brilliant leader, a shrewd politician and a past master at managing his political cohorts.

He was the faction strategist, the dictator of policy, the official spokesman for everything and everybody on his side of the political fence. His word was "all the law and the prophets" to his followers. He was an aggressive man of dynamic personality and

could wither an opponent with a blast of rhetoric. He was feared
— but respected — by his foes.

Therefore when he capitulated to the demands of the GeeGees
and ordered Sheriff Doucet to banish the slot machines, it would
appear that he saw the handwriting on the wall and deemed it the
better part of valor to compromise his authority. The indomitable
leader, who had refused to be dictated to by anyone, was now
being told what to do, and what's more, was doing it.

But the DA lost no time in informing the public that he was
not responsible for the situation. He reminded one and all that the
slots had been brought in before he became district attorney, so
the evil of gambling in the parish could not be laid at his door.

The GeeGees wanted to know: What had been the disposition
of the revenue from the slot machines?

The district attorney was eager to answer. He called a public
meeting and invited both friends and foes. On the speakers' platform were mayors from "all sections of the parish and American
Legion officials" who gave testimony that the "one-armed bandits"
had provided for all sorts of good things in their respective communities; that control of the revenues was in the hands of the
various municipalities.

Members of the school board and police jury present "denied all
accusations of 'bossdom,'" the newspaper stated. Officials who
could not attend the meeting sent letters refuting any hanky-panky.

Thus the proponents of slot machines defended their position on
the issue. Meanwhile the slots were under cover, for the time
being anyway, on orders from the DA. Which elicited another
question from the GeeGees: Had the machine operators been
tipped off?

By mid-September, the crusading anti-administrationists had
organized an all-out effort to oust the courthouse people. The
organization of a Ladies Auxiliary of the Guardians of Good
Government, the first political group for women to be organized
in St. Landry, was announced.

The incumbents' campaign, led by District Attorney Fontenot
and District Judge Guillory, got into full swing in late October.
The lead story in the Herald of October 27 presented the admini-

stration line-up:

"St. Landry's political circle has always been a storm center in Louisiana politics and as the campaign gets underway this week, voters are watching line-ups, candidates, endorsements, and studying the possibilities of combinations and other moves for office that will end up with the Democratic primary January 16.

"Sheriff D. J. Doucet, Clerk of Court Henry Lastrapes and Assessor Lennie Savoy left no doubt in the public mind as to a solid front to present to parish voters in January as they announced the opening of their campaign for Sunset, at the high school auditorium tonight."

(According to one "Cat tale," it was at this Sunset rally that Sheriff Doucet, after making his speech, invited comments from the opposition. There was no immediate response, then a voice from out in the crowd yelled: "I got something to say!" As the fellow made his way to the speaker's platform it was obvious that he was quite drunk, so drunk that he was staggering and incoherent.

"Come right on up, sir!" Cat said cordially, extending a helping hand. "We want everybody to see you!")

The newspaper story also revealed that Mister Austin was again trying his "double harness" strategy, which had worked so well in 1936:

"The lineup is on the same ticket and seeking re-election. At the Sunset meeting two of the candidates for parish coroner are listed as speakers. They are Dr. S. E. Graham, candidate for re-election, and Dr. Lionel Bienvenu.

"Another candidate for election is listed as one of the speakers at the meeting, Remi Sibille, police jury representative of the second ward for several terms.

"On the poster announcing the meeting, which was distributed on the streets of Opelousas and throughout second ward, Sunset being the leading community center, District Attorney L. Austin Fontenot Sr. and District Judge Isom Guillory were on the speaking program, giving St. Landry its first glimpse of a complete St. Landry ticket.

"Definite information on the candidates backed by the Guardians of Good Government was not so readily available, and the line-up of candidates to be backed is yet to be ascertained by the public."

But the GeeGees were campaigning nonetheless. They held meetings at Melville, Port Barre, Sunset, Opelousas, Eunice and Washington. Perhaps they lacked candidates to be "for;" but they had a courthouse full to be "against."

Speakers at GeeGee rallies asked support for Sam Jones, the newspaper reported. No explanation was given as to why the reform group was not backing Vincent Mosely, the St. Landry candidate for governor, who had been one of the prime organizers of the GeeGees.

The political aspic mixed by the GeeGees showed further signs of jelling about the end of October. The newspaper reported:

" . . . candidates paraded before the microphone to talk, appearing more as a ticket than otherwise, but without announced affiliations.

"Candidates introducing themselves and asking support were Dudley Briley, Simon Stelly and Maxile Savoy, for sheriff; Dr. J. W. Pittman, for coroner; Bean Bag Strother, senate; and for legislature, D. M. Pellerin, Francis Edwards and Dr. Duplechin. While the Guardians of Good Government have no candidates they reserve the right to endorse candidates. Politically inclined had reported, generally, that the candidates appearing at the meeting were all on the same side."

(The "Bean Bag Strother" appelation for the GeeGee-endorsed candidate for the senate must have brought appreciative chuckles from the opposition. "Bean Bag" was the name derisively applied to Howard Strother, editor of the New Era of Eunice, by J. N. Langford, fiery editor of the Opelousas Herald)

The people who were looking out the courthouse windows in 1940 were the same ones who were on the outside looking in four years earlier. Except for one man — Henry Lastrapes, clerk of court, the only anti-Long man who had been returned to parish office in the 1936 election.

In 1936 it had been the "Home Rulers" versus "The Machine." Now the parish administration was being challenged by the same political foes under a new name, Guardians of Good Government. Austin Fontenot labeled the GeeGees "ancient political foes," the same ones, he said, who had fought him in previous years.

Every parish office was contested. Sheriff Doucet had three opponents: his former "double harness" team mate, Dudley Briley; Maxile Savoy of Eunice and Simon Stelly, whom he had defeated in 1936.

Lennie Savoy, the assessor, was opposed by Garland L. Dejean, of a prominent St. Landry family; Clerk of Court Lastrapes had an equally formidable opponent, Paul D. Pavy Sr. There were four candidates for coroner: the incumbent, Dr. Graham; Dr. Lionel J. Bienvenu, Dr. J. L. Pittman and Dr. J. J. Stagg.

The courthouse boys got themselves a name also, the "Fair Government" ticket. Both the "Fairs" and the "Goods" scheduled meetings in all sections of the parish and harangued the voters in both French and English. The Opelousas newspaper gave the two sides equal time — almost. Observant readers could note that the "Fairs" usually got a few more column inches than the "Goods."

Reporting on opening rallies by the two factions, the newspaper cautiously separated the sheep from the goats:

"Different in presentation (from the Gee Gees), the Fair Government candidates met Friday night to tell Second Ward voters of the accomplishments of the present parish administration seeking re-election.

"Sheriff D. J. Doucet told of appointment of deputies in every section of the parish and announced that proper supervision at dances, and other public gatherings had resulted in only one major murder crime in the parish during the past three and one half years.

"Clerk of Court Henry Lastrapes explained the functions of his office and pointed to the harmony resulting from public service. He said that no man had ever been able to criticize honestly the manner in which he had run his office. His deputies, he said, were efficient and represented a selection that had taken years to make.

"Assessor Lennie Savoy called attention to voters that homestead exemptions had increased from near the 2,000 mark to over 5,000 since he took office. He announced that the annual savings to home owners this year, because of this increase, amounted to approximately $119,000 . . . .

"District Attorney L. Austin Fontenot, who acted as chairman, said that taxpayers had been saved thousands of dollars as a result of the perfect work of Sheriff Doucet in working up evidence where charges had been made, the result being no long criminal court sessions."

Judge Guillory spoke on behalf of the "ins," as did candidates for other parish offices on the Doucet ticket. The paper reported that Eloi Guillory, Eunice candidate for the senate on the "Fair" ticket, was unable to be present because of "pressing business in winding up details of the recently closed Tri-Parish Fair, of which he is secretary."

Thus voters learned that the courthouse boys had won over to their side two valuable allies: Clerk of Court Lastrapes, the only parish official the Long machine couldn't beat in 1936, and Eloi Guillory, kinsman of Judge Isom Guillory, and one of the Eunice area's most popular public figures. Eloi had been on the other side in 1936.

Overshadowing the 1940 election campaign in St. Landry was a hot potato of a hassle between the editors of the two parish newspapers, the Opelousas Herald and the Eunice New Era. The feuding had begun in 1936 when the Opelousas editor was anti-Long and the Eunice editor was pro-Long. Now their positions were reversed.

The editor of the Eunice paper seemed to be especially gifted at invective and innuendo, the Opelousas editor responded with disparagement calculated to tear the other sheet to pieces. The air was blue with epithets: "fence hopping," "two-faced," "slimy, snarling, filthy-tail," "nincompoop, Jackpot, Earl Long stooges," "lower than a whale stool in the ocean," etcetera, etcetera.

The Opelousas editor found the editorials printed in the New Era "of a lambasting nature, making charges and insinuations where assertions could not be backed up by proof." Such accusations, he wrote, were "a throw-back to the dark ages in conception, thought and expression." The battle of the editors ended up in the courts.

The GeeGees turned their guns on the district attorney. One accusation concerned a road, built by WPA labor, that was said to lead to the DA's own private lake and camp. Another alleged that the grand jury, called into session in November, was composed of "administration men."

These allegations Mister Austin vehemently denied. In the case of the road, he called up officials to support his explanation that the WPA road was surveyed to Second Lake Pleasure Club, a hunting lodge that was operated by an organization which had for its president an active member of the "Goods" and a former Home Ruler, Veazie Pavy. And what was more, the DA continued, the project had been designed to give work to the unemployed in the Melville-Palmetto area.

As for the grand jury, Austin said that no matter who was serving, that body was going to probe every complaint of alleged violations of the law, "and that includes dual office holding, dead-heads, slot machines and every other form of crime."

Six weeks before the election, the Eunice editor, indicted by the grand jury on charges of libel and slander, did a little charging of his own. He charged the district judge, the district attorney and the sheriff "had failed to perform their required duties in connection with shutting down on slot machines in St. Landry Parish."

The state attorney general himself said he would investigate the charges. This dignitary was one Lessley P. Gardiner, destined to become one of St. Landry's most eminent jurists, also destined to figure importantly in the life of D. J. "Cat" Doucet.

The printed name-calling and mud-slinging of that election year set a precedent even for St. Landry Parish. The new-born daily tabloid newspaper in the parish, the Opelousas Daily World, took no sides; after the battle smoke had abated, the editor proudly announced that the paper had received a journalistic award for remaining neutral.

Just before the primary election, the Opelousas Herald editor jumped off the fence. Editorially, the newspaper endorsed the "courthouse boys," Lastrapes, Savoy and Doucet. No other candidates' names were mentioned. The editorial asked citizens to "not only support but vote for Doucet, Lastrapes and Savoy next Tuesday."

The editor pointed out that the courthouse candidates had not used the tactics employed by their opponents, the GeeGees:

"No one has ever heard Clerk of Court Henry Lastrapes talk in this manner. Assessor Lennie Savoy's mouth has never and would not utter such descriptions of an opponent. Sheriff D. J. Doucet's campaign has always been clean. These three men have spoken from the platform in every St. Landry community but no such remarks have ever come from their lips."

At the final administration rally the candidates promised "a continuance of the principles of the late Huey Long and the principles and benefits carried on during the past four years of office." Mister Austin claimed that "every charge made by the opposition has been disproven."

The GeeGees continued to the end to maintain that they had endorsed no other candidate except Sam Jones for governor. "Mr. Stelly, Mr. Briley and Mr. Maxile Savoy are all three good, honest men," the GeeGee circular stated, "and have agreed to offer their candidacies to the people from the same platform."

And Cat continued to maintain that his opponents "had three horses in the race."

Election day dawned bright and clear. A record vote was predicted; some 16,000 persons had registered to vote. Some of the voters who streamed in to the polls that day were about to switch allegiance. Some erstwhile staunch supporters of the Long regime were having second thoughts, with every newspaper filled with stories about former Long leaders being probed, investigated, convicted of charges of embezzlement, theft, malfeasance in office.

Two of the courthouse boys survived the purge. Clerk of Court Lastrapes and Assessor Lennie Savoy were returned to office by wide margins.

Sheriff Cat ran up 6,270 votes, but the combined votes given his three opponents totaled 6,493. The sheriff was short 223 votes for a majority. The issue would be decided in the second primary, set for February 20, when Cat would face his old enemy, Simon

The Cat and St. Landry

Stelly.

The week following the election the parish was in the grip of the coldest weather in 40 years. Within a few hours the temperature plummeted to the low 20's; sleet and snow covered everything for the better part of two weeks. Faucets left running created the danger of water shortages; natural gas consumption went up to eight times more than usual. Schools were closed, business was at a standstill. Even politics cooled down.

The warm-up in the weather coincided with a fevered effort to preserve the status quo in the courthouse. Cat was on the defensive, replying to radio attacks made by the GeeGees. Speaking at an Arnaudville rally, Cat said he had never before offered any criticism of his opponents, and if he to stoop so low as to criticize the wives and children of the candidates, like the opposition was doing, he did not want any political office.

"I got twice as many votes as Simon in the first primary," he reminded his Arnaudville audience. "And I'm gonna do it again!" Loud applause.

"They said I'm not fit to be sheriff!" He challenged his opponents to "show me some women and children they bought medicine for, or taken to the hospital, or bought a casket for." If this could be done, "I'll get out the race!"

Cat also answered charges that his deputies had been made to kick back money from salary checks for his campaign.

"That deputy they took to New Orleans to make a statement to the FBI, they made him do that!" he declared.

Howcome Sam Jones could "write to everybody in the state and beg for campaign funds," he wanted to know. And he, the sheriff, and all the postmasters had to contribute to President Roosevelt's campaign fund. "But it's a penitentiary offense if my deputies contribute to mine!"

Candidates for major offices in the run-off included Cat and Simon Stelly, for sheriff; Henry D. Larcade Jr. and Dr. J. A. Duplechin, state legislature; Eloi Guillory and Nat J. Amy, state senate; Dr. Lionel J. Bienvenu and Dr. J. J. Stagg, coroner.

Four days before the second primary, the Opelousas Herald announced support of the other administration candidates, Henry

Larcade, Eloi Guillory and Dr. Bienvenu, and added a plug for Sheriff Doucet.

(Oscar Guidry of Church Point, a long-time Long man, had already won one of the two senate seats in the 16th senatorial district, composed of St. Landry and Acadia. Eloi Guillory had led his two opponents in both parishes in the first primary, having a combined vote of 10,243; 5,492 in St. Landry and 4,751 in Acadia. The run-off pitted Eloi against another Eunice man, Nat Amy. Two of the other anti-administration candidates were also Eunice citizens, Dr. J. A. Duplechin, a well known dentist, and Dr. Stagg, physician and surgeon, and member of a prominent St. Landry family).

The newspaper endorsement had words of glowing praise for Eloi, one of the most popular and well-liked personalities of his day:

"Eloi Guillory . . . is as plain as an old shoe, as comfortable in meeting and talking to as your closest friend, as smart as a whip, and with a long record of service. Eloi knows St. Landry, knows our needs, and has the initiative and personality to go after it."

The editor quoted a humorously exaggerated speculation made by Eloi about his opponent:

"You know what would happen if that fellow got elected? The first thing he would do is get the capitol moved to Eunice. And you know we haven't got a place big enough for that 24-story building!"

The editor labeled Henry Larcade (who later became United States congressman) "one of the more experienced community builders of St. Landry, which is to say of Louisiana. He has always been predominantly identified with the promotion of the parish for over 20 years. His past experience adequately fits him for further service. He is human. He is approachable. He is energetic . . . ."

For Cat, the editor saved some of his warmest words:

"Cat Doucet has been sheriff for the past four years. During this period the parish has enjoyed the most peaceful respite from law violations in the over 200 years of southwest Louisiana history.

69

His office has been run efficiently and all records have been found by auditors to be in perfect order. 'Cat' is easily met. He is of St. Landry and his ambition is to serve his people.

"High or low, low or high, any and every citizen of the parish can walk up to any one of these three men and talk over a problem and it isn't necessary to take off your hat and bow and scrape . . . . "

But the handwriting on the wall had turned into block letters. The pendulum had swung too far in the other direction. There was no way . . . .

Cat Doucet lost out to Simon Stelly by 257 votes. Doucet polled 6,338, Stelly 6,595.

Cat's star, which had risen brightly with that of Huey Long, had now gone into eclipse with the downfall of the Kingfish's brother Earl. The eclipse was to last for 12 years . . .

The day after the run-off, Cat gave out prepared statements to the newspapers. It was the usual type statement given the press by a defeated candidate, and was printed in all parish newspapers, including the new daily, the Daily World. After the text of the statement was given, the Daily World writer added a fillip:

"Informally, Doucet asked that the World 'make it plain that I'm not mad at anyone.'"

The new paper put out an extra the day after election. The election run-down began like this:

"St. Landry voters joined the remainder of the state Tuesday in sweeping clean the halls of government, refusing to send back a single state or parish administration official faced by an anti-administration opponent in the run-off primary.

"Most spectacular defeat of the election was that of D. J. 'Cat' Doucet, sheriff, who was nosed out by Simon Stelly who had the backing of the Good Government League, the Jones forces and the anti-administration group in general."

Some three months later, when the new sheriff was about to take office, the old sheriff had another statement in the Daily World:

"Before the election I was a friend of the newly-elected sheriff and I am sure that he knows that I'll always be his friend. I hold no malice towards anyone. My only hope is that St. Landry will continue to forge forward for the good of the people."

Several days later the same newspaper carried this provocative headline:

"St. Landry Has Two Sheriffs; Doucet Agrees to Stay Until End of Month to Help Stelly Get Settled."

That headline must have startled a great many readers, certainly those who remembered all the harsh words uttered during the bitter campaign. The story explained the bizarre situation, also provided readers with a chuckle or two:

"There was confusion in the sheriff's office this morning. Two sheriffs.

"New Sheriff Simon Stelly took his oath of office late Monday afternoon, outgoing Sheriff D. J. 'Cat' Doucet's term is not quite over. So they're both there, getting along well . . .

"Sheriff Stelly's new force has been sworn in and reported for duty this morning.

"At 10 o'clock this morning Sheriff Doucet and his force were sitting along the wall at the rear of the office. Sheriff Stelly's force were ranging around the suites getting acquainted.

"Every time one of the new deputies wanted a rubber band or a stamp, one of the old force would get up and get it for him . . .

"Whatever disagreements might have arisen over the situation have been squelched, however, as new Sheriff Stelly made an agreement with old Sheriff Doucet that the latter's force will stay on duty, along with the new force, until the end of the month, which comes in mighty handy for Sheriff Stelly.

"The new sheriff is taking office at a bad time — he has the grand jury and all the witnesses on hand, a tax sale . . . "

7

The Case Against Cat

Cat's enemies were not through with him. During 1941 Cat made more news headlines than he had throughout his four years as sheriff.

The case against Cat started in November of 1940 when the State of Louisiana filed suit against him and his bonding company for $25,473.30. The suit followed a one-day investigation by the newly set-up Louisiana Crime Commission.

Legal counsel for Cat and the bonding company denied the alleged irregularities, which included: official property not turned over, $1,304.30; unsupported cash withdrawals from the sheriff's salary fund, $9,571.85; cash disbursed from the salary fund to deputies in addition to their regular salaries, $14,690; duplicated withdrawals for transporting prisoners and insane, $50.55.

Cat defended himself in a public statement. He said that he had received his quietus; that he had been advised by letter that his settlements with the state auditor had been audited and found correct.

As for the bonuses to the deputies, this had been done with the approval, in writing, of proper authorities. Deputies had started out on small salaries, with the understanding that they would be compensated when sufficient funds had accumulated.

Authority to pay the back salary, and the amounts to be paid, had come from the Louisiana State Police at Baton Rouge, Cat averred. The letter authorizing the payments had been placed on file in the sheriff's office and left there.

The former sheriff pointed out that the investigation into his affairs was "under the absolute control of those whom I politically opposed in the last state campaign."

One of the complaints against Cat was that he had made "excessive charges" in the line of duty while searching for Lester Senegal, who had murdered a Sunset peace officer, Gabriel Burleigh. The search for Senegal had gone on for more than two years. Also under scrutiny was pay for extra deputies to serve at the Tri-Parish Fair in Eunice.

"It may look funny now," Cat stated, "but at the time people were demanding that I track down the killer at all costs, and deputies were asked at the Eunice fair because the school children of Evangeline, Acadia and St. Landry were being brought there in busses by the thousands. It did not then, nor now, appear to me to be either excessive or vain."

(The statement, of course, was written by Old Man Austin. It did not include the fact that a man from the St. Landry Sheriff's Department had been posted in a Beaumont, Texas hotel for two years, checking out tips that Senegal was hiding in the vicinity. The case ended when a Texas lawman, acting on a tip from Sheriff Doucet, located Senegal and attempted to arrest him. When the Negro attacked the lawman with an ax, the officer shot him. The Texas officer collected the sizable reward offered by Sheriff Doucet and the St. Landry Parish Police Jury. The body of Senegal was brought back, and on orders from the sheriff, was put on display, in the casket, in the Opelousas courthouse for three days so that all could see that the murderer of Marshal Burleigh had been apprehended).

Twenty-seven former deputies who had served with Cat were interrogated at the Crime Commission hearing. Seven of these said they had given their bonus checks back to the sheriff; some of the remainder testified they had contributed some of their back pay to the campaign fund, others said they had given nothing.

A number of Cat's former deputies substantiated his statement that at the time they were employed the sheriff had told them he was not aware of what his salary fund would be, and he would start them at small salaries, with the understanding that at the end of the fiscal year, should there be anything left in the sheriff's fund, he would give them bonuses.

The Crime Commission's probe in St. Landry was not particularly shocking to citizens. Investigations were the order of the day; parish and federal grand juries were indicting officials right and left, some were already in prison. Charges of "irregularities" had reached epidemic stage in all corners of the state.

73

The Cat and St. Landry

The Louisiana electorate voted November 5, 1940 on 28 new amendments proposed by the new legislature. One of the amendments provided that the offices of district judge and district attorney in St. Landry be vacated, and an election called to fill the vacancies.

And, as Cat Doucet would phrase it, "that's how the opposition got rid of Isom and Mister Austin." Both Judge Guillory and District Attorney wielded too much power to be left in office.

Both the unseated officials made attempts to retain their offices. District Attorney Fontenot qualified to run in the election, but withdrew at the last minute. Judge Guillory eventually lost his legal fight to keep the district judgeship.

Cat didn't have a friend left in office. The new sheriff, the new district judge and the new district attorney, plus every official in state office, were anti-Long and anti-Cat.

The former sheriff's attorneys were gathering ammunition to fight the charges against their client. Cat's vouchers came up missing. The amount of money represented by the vouchers was better than $9,000, the alleged "unsupported withdrawals from the sheriff's salary fund." A representative of the Crime Commission had come to Opelousas, picked up the vouchers, which had been filed by Cat in the sheriff's office, and took them to Baton Rouge for photographing. Defense attorneys demanded the return of the vouchers.

Attorneys for the bonding company claimed that the company could not be sued under the tax collector's bond, since Cat had been cleared as tax collector. The bonding company had $26,000 on Cat; $6,000 as sheriff, and $20,000 as tax collector.

The bonding company declared that the official property which had not been turned over to the succeeding sheriff, amounting to $1,304, were badges usually kept by deputies, and guns and equipment lost by Doucet through no negligence on his part.

An automobile in question, which was alleged not to have been turned over to the succeeding sheriff, was the personal property of one of Cat's deputies before he took the job.

The bonding company further stated that the former sheriff had attached to each warrant of withdrawal an itemized account of the items covered thereby, which itemized account was submitted and attached to the warrant.

These records were kept intact so long as Doucet was in office, the company lawyers averred, but upon leaving office the records were turned over to his successor and in some manner some of the vouchers attached to the warrants were apparently lost.

The attorneys concurred with Cat's explanation of the $14,000 bonuses given deputies. This method, the bonding people pointed out, had been approved by the Bureau of Criminal Investigation and the office of the Supervisor of Public Accounts during Cat's entire term.

Not to be confounded, the Cat's enemies continued in howling pursuit. During the "spring clean-up" of 1941, the district attorney asked a probe of the audit of the former sheriff's books. The former sheriff was indicted by the grand jury on 30 counts, all charging embezzlement of public funds. Amount of money involved was $4,245.

The investigative spotlight was turned on other top parish officials, also the police jury and Opelousas city officials.

Caught between two fires, the Cat was having his hide well singed. On one hand the civil suit evolving from the crime commission's one-day probe, on the other the grand jury indictments.

Defense attorneys challenged the constitutionality of the legislative act which had created the Louisiana Crime Commission. They threw other bolts into the legal machinery; the district judge, an acknowledged anti-Cat, was asked to recuse himself from the case involving the civil suit stemming from the crime commission's investigation. This was granted.

After Cat's indictment by the grand jury, his attorneys again asked for another judge to sit on this case. The matter was left up to an out-of-parish judge, who ruled against the petition. Eventually, the state supreme court asked the judge to recuse himself, and Judge Iris Dupont of Iberville Parish was named to try the case.

Cat still had a cheering section.

After his indictment, bond for Cat was set for $1,800. Immediately Morgan Goudeau Sr., a prominent planter of the

Melville area, stepped forward to sign the bond.

In a newspaper statement the same day, Cat asked his constituents to withhold judgment until he had a chance to have his say. He also expressed his thanks:

"In the meantime I want to thank, from the bottom of my heart, the men and women of St. Landry who have telephoned me and sent me messages during the last few hours, of their best wishes and belief in my sincerity and honesty. I particularly want to thank the splendid men who swarmed the courthouse this morning for the purpose of seeking to be one of my bondsmen."

In May of 1941, the Doucet attorneys in the civil suit, George Wallace and Wade O. Martin Jr., asked for a trial by jury. The request was granted, and the judge set Cat's bond for $1,000.

Later that month Cat pleaded "not guilty" to the grand jury indictments and asked for an early trial. His request was denied. The judge indicated that the court could not interfere with the district attorney in the fixing of cases as to whom should be called and when. Also, the term of the petit jury was to expire the next day, which would indicate that to have a trial at a time other than the regular fall term would necessitate a special term of the petit jury.

Representing Cat in this case were Judge Allen Bordelon of Marksville, in Avoyelles Parish, and Lessley P. Gardiner, the former attorney general, now practicing law in Opelousas.

In mid-July, the grand jury indicted Cat on one more count, charging embezzlement of $3,274.06 in public funds. The alleged misuse of public funds in this amount was "unlawfully expended for purchases of gas and oil, automobile parts and supplies for persons other than the sheriff and his deputies."

This last indictment, number 31, was not consistent with a statement made two months before by the district attorney. In a statement printed in the newspaper, the district attorney had explained why the 30 indictments by the grand jury involved only some $4,000, when the crime commission had alleged that better than $25,000 in funds from the sheriff's department had been improperly accounted for.

Citing the article number of the Criminal Code, the prosecutor had explained that a person convicted of misuse of public funds, whether the amount be $1 or $25,000, the penalty would be the same: restitution of the money, and the person convicted "shall be imprisoned at hard labor, for not less than six months, and not more than five years."

Therefore, the DA's statement continued, to save the grand jury time and effort, the body had been asked to probe only part of the whole matter.

But the district attorney did dig deeper, and came up with another indictment. The Doucet bond, this time around, was set at $900.

Cat had claimed that the vouchers in question — the itemized statements attached to each warrant — had "in some manner, been lost." By October the other side had some explaining to do. Important records in the case, including the original indictment returned by the grand jury, had been "lost, mislaid or stolen," they said.

The missing documents had been left on the judge's desk. Later it was discovered that the records had been filed incorrectly.

The political alignments of the jury commission and the grand jury which had indicted Cat came under fire from the defense lawyers. They charged the jury commission had been "hand-picked" and the grand jury "stacked." The prosecution claimed that former district attorney Austin Fontenot and former judge Isom Guillory were acting as ex-officio counsel for the defense; the defense charged that not only were members of the jury commission and grand jury anti-Cat, but most of the witnesses called were his political foes also.

It took the bombing of Pearl Harbor to get Cat Doucet's name off front page . . .

The case dragged out for four years. Defense attorneys went to the supreme court four times for rulings. Meanwhile the charges of wrongdoing on the part of Opelousas city officials had been cleared up; parish officials under indictment on charges of embezzlement had been exonerated by due process of law. Some of the old wounds had begun to heal, some foes had become friends.

77

Finally, Cat's attorneys found the opposition napping. Time had run out. The plea of prescription was entered, and the judge nolle prossed the case.

Looking back, Cat commented: "They said I stole the whole parish!" He talks about those troublesome times without rancor or bitterness, but every now and then a little bit of the sweet wine of victory adds zest to the telling:

"They said I had unsupported vouchers. It was them that unsupported my vouchers! Judge Dupont said in court that I had to be shown those vouchers. So him and me and Lessley, we went in the office. I knew darn well they had receipts on the vouchers. You had to put receipts on them. You can't charge $100 - $125 to go somewhere and don't have no hotel receipt or nothing.

"So I looked at them and showed them to Lessley. 'You see them two little holes there?' I said. 'If that's what they've got me indicted for, they ain't got a damn thing!'"

"Them two little holes" in the vouchers were the marks left by wire staples, which showed, Cat said, that the itemized statements had been attached, according to proper procedure, then later detached.

"We showed that to Judge Dupont. He throwed 'em out as fast as we brought 'em in!"

Then there was the matter of "them little old tin badges." Cat tells about this with contemptuous snorts:

"They even had me charged, indicted, for them little old tin badges I had give to special deputies. To keep peace at the dance halls and honky-tonks. They cost about $1.35 a piece. And when Simon beat me they indicted me for two-three dozen of them badges that my boys didn't bring back. Half of them kept the badges for souvenirs, most of them lost 'em. And they were cheap and they'd break — they were made like a diaper pin welded on a piece of tin."

That was the way it was: the ups and down of politics, the name of the game. Something that had to be endured and reckoned with at the time and thereafter forgotten.

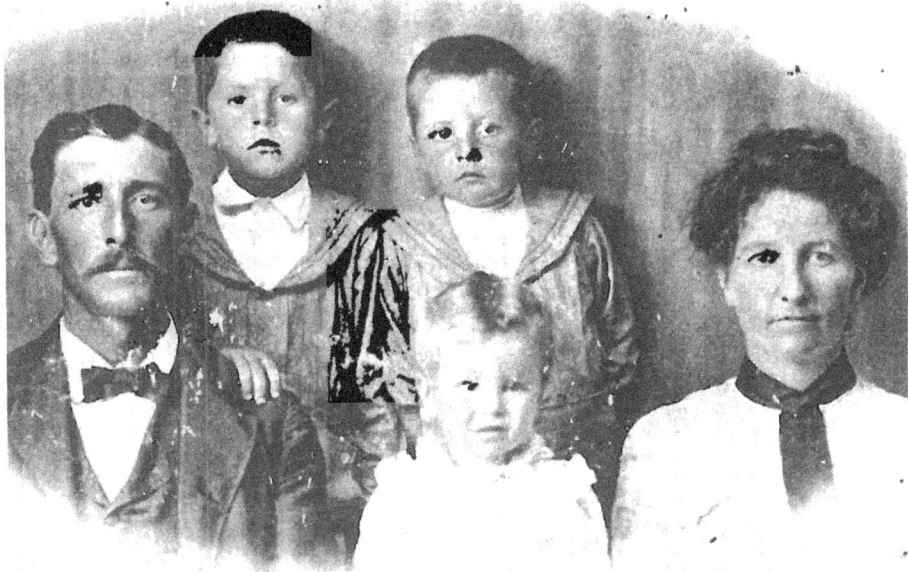

Lucius and Aza Lafleur Doucet and their three sons: Hosea, Daly Joseph and Elton. (Photo courtesy Elton Doucet family)

Teen-age Cat Doucet, seated, right, and an unidentified companion. (Photo courtesy Yvonne Doucet Fontenot)

Birthplace of Cat Doucet in the Grand Prairie community of St. Landry Parish.

(Fontenot photo)

A "back when" snapshot shows Cat Doucet near the tomb of George Washington. The trip to the nation's capital was made with L. Austin Fontenot Sr. about 1928.

Side view of front "galerie" of Acadian-type house. (Fontenot photo)

The newlyweds, Cat and Anna, honeymooned in Hot Springs, Arkansas.

D. J. "Cat" Doucet, in a photograph taken during his first term
of office as sheriff of St. Landry Parish, 1936-1940.

The Cat and his friends: with Rene Derouen (top, left), Louisiana congressman, in Washington; with "Te Nonc" Homer
Dupre (lower left), Regile Doucet's father-in-law; above, with
a cowboy-hatted friend, Johnny Hoffman.

❖   ❖   ❖

St. Landry Parish Courthouse forms an impressive backdrop for Sheriff Doucet and his deputy son Harold. When Harold was elected Opelousas chief of police, the father-son law enforcement team became known as "the Cat and the Kitten."   (J. A. Bourdier photo)

DOUCET TICKET THROWS IN HAT — D. J. (Cat) Doucet, left, and two members of his ticket discuss the forthcoming Democratic primary as they waited yesterday to file qualifications. With Doucet are Mrs. R. S. Parrott of Eunice and Edward V. (Dud) Pavy, while at left is Wilfred Kidder of Arnaudville. All three qualified as candidates for the house of representatives.

Doucet-Parrott ticket, 1952

The Doucet-Savoy bandwagon. Replica of the cat carries the campaign slogan, "Cat's the Man!"

A Baton Rouge TV newsman interviews the sheriff of
St. Landry on the Civil Rights controversy. Cat became
involved in several state-wide hassles over racial issues.

❧

Sheriff Doucet, in a Daily World photo taken during his
last term of office, 1964-1968.

❧

The Cat and the Captain. Here Sheriff Doucet and Capt. E. N. Gabarino of Troop K, State Police, seem to be in affable agreement.

A truckload of gambling devices is unloaded onto the St. Landry Parish courthouse square. The Daily World building on Market Street is in background.   (Daily World Photo)

✣

"They can't put the Cat out!"
(J. A. Bourdier photo)

"LET'S
KEEP
NO. 'CAT' 118
OUR
SHERIFF"

Election — Nov. 4, 1967

The 1967 campaign card.

After 12 years, he came back strong. Man in dark
sweater is the sheriff-elect's son-in-law, Jerrel Fontenot.
(Photo reproduced from Daily World of Feb. 20, 1952)

The 1964 "victory smile" was expansive. Cat shares the spotlight with a running mate, Senator-elect Austin J. Fontenot. (Daily World photo)

⚜   ⚜

"We talked French," said Cat Doucet, right, after he visited with Charles de Gaulle, President of France, in 1960. At left is Morgan Goudeau III of Opelousas.

Former sheriff Cat Doucet in 1971. The "old sheriff" was one of the St. Landry officials interviewed by T. Harry Williams for material for his Pulitzer-prize winning biography of Huey Long.   (Fontenot photo)

8

Footsteps On The Stairway

Came 1944, another election, another sheriff. This time Clayton Guilbeau, who had just completed a four-year term in the Louisiana Legislature, elected to that office on the anti-Long ticket.

"I wanted to run that time," Cat said. "But Mister Austin wouldn't let me. He told me: 'We'll run one of them, one from the other side, and he'll beat Simon Stelly. Then you can get in there and beat him.'"

When Sheriff Guilbeau took office in May, 1944, the first thing that he did was announce that his chief deputy would be one D. J. "Cat" Doucet (Cat was still under indictment; all during the 1944 campaign and for some time thereafter the case see-sawed back and forth between the district court and the supreme court).

Just before the new sheriff took over, the district attorney ordered old sheriff Simon Stelly to "smash all slot machines and close up gambling in the parish."

The slots had sneaked back into St. Landry — right under the noses of those who had made such an issue of the gambling machines in the previous campaign.

Deputy Cat figured in several news stories originating from the sheriff's department. One story related that he was one of a group of officers sent to Lake Providence to fetch three men and three women arrested there in connection with the robbery of the W. R. Clopton Store of Morrow, in St. Landry. One of the women brought to the St. Landry jail was said to be Marie Barrow, the wife of the gang leader and sister of the notorious outlaw, Clyde Barrow. Another time Cat apprehended a fugitive. The story in the Daily World was headlined: "Picture Is Bad News for Fugitive; Doucet Nabs Him Second Time." Above the story was a picture of Cat, alongside a picture of the captured fugitive.

The newspaper story elaborated on the second-time-around capture:

The Cat and St. Landry

"Sunday night, for the second time in less than two years, Mervin Persilver, a twice-escaped convict, met Deputy Sheriff D. J. 'Cat' Doucet, and, as a result, for the second time found himself in the state penitentiary at Angola, this time the Daily World aiding in locating the fugitive."

A year before Persilver had escaped from a Florida prison where he was serving a life sentence for murder. He made his way to St. Landry Parish, robbed and beat a Krotz Springs resident, and took to the Atchafalaya swamps. He was apprehended by Deputy Doucet on an island in the Atchafalaya River "after a long and frigid chase" ("I nearly froze to death," says Cat), and returned to Angola for a 10-year term.

But Angola couldn't hold him either. After his escape from the Louisiana prison the Daily World published his picture. Some Port Barre residents recognized the fugitive from the newspaper picture and notified the sheriff's department that Persilver was in a Port Barre cafe.

" . . . Doucet hustled out to the scene, only half expecting to find Persilver because numerous tips have been chased down recently, to no avail.

"When he walked in he recognized the man, pulled his gun and made the arrest. Persilver was armed with a .38 caliber six-shooter but made no attempt to use it."

These were the "beginning of the end" years. News columns were filled with stories about St. Landry men in service; so many lost their lives, many were prisoners of war. Louisiana had a "singing governor," Jimmie Davis; Louisiana schools added a 12th grade, citizens were making "victory gardens" and knitting for the Red Cross, school children were collecting scrap metal and paper for the war effort.

Cat worked at his deputy job until the end of May, 1947, when he resigned to start campaigning for sheriff (On the state scene, chief contenders for the governor's office were ancient opponents of eight years back: Sam Jones, whose election in 1940 had set off the "sweeping reforms," and Earl Long, doggedly making his way

80

back to the governor's mansion).

When Cat announced for sheriff, he bolted his faction. "Old Man Austin" and his former ticket mates were committed to the incumbent, Sheriff Clayton Guilbeau, so his erstwhile friends became his political foes.

In addition to Cat and Sheriff Guilbeau, three other candidates announced for sheriff: Dudley Briley, former sheriff Simon Stelly and Roland Chachere, Opelousas chief of police. Later Briley withdrew and gave his support to Stelly. Then Stelly withdrew, leaving three in the running: former sheriff Doucet, Sheriff Guilbeau and Chief Roland Chachere.

Stelly's withdrawal, according to a statement given the press, was done "in the interest of good government and the election of Sam Jones as governor." Chief Chachere, the paper said, had been campaigning with the same political support as Stelly — the adherents of Jones in the parish.

A few weeks later found the factions lining up. The Good Government ticket (no longer known in the press as the "Gee Gees") listed the following:

Roland Chachere for sheriff; Lee Mizzi, clerk of court; Dudley Lastrapes, assessor; Robert Dejean, Walter Champagne Jr., and Felix Dejean Jr., representatives; Dr. Whyte Owen, coroner, and Simon Stelly, senator.

The Independents, headed by Sheriff Clayton Guilbeau, were Henry Lastrapes and Lennie Savoy, seeking re-election to their respective offices of clerk of court and assessor; Dr. Gerald Bertinot for coroner; Ed Dubuisson, Howard Lafleur and Sidney Sylvester, representatives; Lessley P. Gardiner, senator.

Cat headed the other party. This was the "no name" party, simply known in the press as "the third party." On Cat's ticket were Louis Fontenot for clerk of court; J. B. Lewis, assessor; Eli Ardoin, Rene Young and Clyde Doucet, representatives; Wilson Moosa, senator.

The Good Government ticket sided with Sam Jones, the Independents declared they were what the faction title implied, independent. Cat and his ticket mates said they were for Uncle Earl.

And Uncle Earl was for Cat. He came to town to make a speech

The Cat and St. Landry

and asked support for Cat Doucet.

About the time the campaign was picking up momentum Cat got some bad publicity. The newspaper reported he had been hailed into city court and fined $7.50 for fighting.

Cat and Sam "Lefty" Tarleton, at that time sports announcer for KSLO, the Opelousas radio station, had an altercation on the street in front of the radio station. Police Chief Chachere had charged the two with disturbing the peace.

Both Cat and Lefty pleaded "not guilty." Cat told City Judge Lee Mizzi he had paid for a political announcement that had not been used. Lefty said Cat had no business going to the boss to complain without grounds. The fight, the paper said, "followed an exchange of heated words."

Cat admits that he hit Lefty first. "He shot off his mouth and I hit him. He hit me back. He was left-handed you know. That's why they called him Lefty, when he was a ball player. He used to write for the Daily World. Last I heard he was working for the Lake Charles paper. We're still friends. We just passed a few blows. I liked to fight when I was young."

Earl Long got to be governor, but Cat didn't get to be sheriff.

When the first primary votes were counted, Sheriff Guilbeau was on top with 6,447. Roland Chachere was second man with 5,456, and Cat the third party man, was third with 4,966.

The only Cat candidate to get in the run-off was Louis Fontenot, running for clerk of court. Shortly after the primary Fontenot withdrew, giving the office without contest to veteran Henry Lastrapes.

Since Cat couldn't lick his old buddies, he joined 'em. He threw his support to the Independents, who lost their independence altogether — they came out for Earl Long.

The joint forces of the Independents and Cat's third party succeeded in re-electing Sheriff Guilbeau. Assessor Lennie Savoy was also returned to office, and Lessley P. Gardiner was the new state senator from St. Landry. The three candidates for state legislature on the Independent ticket, Edward Dubuisson, Howard Lafleur and Sidney Sylvester, were also victorious.

Speculation among members of the opposing faction was that Cat's "third party" had been set up, in the first place, by Austin

Fontenot as another brilliant piece of political trickery, a move calculated to divide the vote in the first primary. Louis Fontenot's subsequent withdrawal, plus the coalition of the third party and the Independents, plus the joint support of Earl Long, supported the speculations.

Newspapers of the period reflected the changing times, foreshadowed things to come:

During 1949 a group of Negro residents of St. Landry signed a petition that was filed in federal court, asking for equal educational facilities . . . one of the big news stories was the execution, in a portable electric chair set up in the St. Landry courthouse, of two Negroes, the Cook brothers, who had confessed to the murder of a retired Naval officer and assault on his woman companion . . . Edward Honeycutt, facing execution for the rape of a Eunice woman, was taken from the St. Landry jail by three parish men. While they flipped a coin to see which one would kill him, the Negro escaped by diving into the Atchafalaya River, was later found clinging to a tree in the river and returned to jail.

A bizarre footnote to the execution of the Cook brothers was provided by the Rev. A. W. Rosette, the Negro Baptist preacher who had attended the Elgie Stephens' hanging. Rosette visited frequently with the Cook brothers in the parish jail while the two were awaiting execution, he related.

"One of them was ready to be a Christian," Rosette said. "I baptized him in jail, in the bathtub. But the other brother resisted. He refused Christianity. But I kept on anyway. And I was there for the execution. Those days they had a portable electric chair in Baton Rouge, and when it was time for a condemned man to die, the state executioner would bring the electric chair to the parish."

The electric chair was brought to the St. Landry courthouse for the execution of the condemned brothers. Rosette said he wore a new Prince Albert coat, one that he had purchased to replace the one ruined in 1939 when he caught Elgie Stephens' body after the rope was cut.

"I prayed over those boys," Rosette said. "Right up to the last minute. The Christian one joined in the prayers, the other one didn't. The state executioner was a hard man; before we could finish the praying he said to me: 'Get on with it. I've got to get my job done.'

"I told him: 'the Lord will reckon with you. You're a cruel man, a hard man. This is just another job to you. These boys are going to die for what they've done. Can't you give them time to get ready to meet the Lord?'"

The execution over, again Rev. Rosette officiated as he had done for Stephens.

"I helped get their bodies out the chair," he said. "The smell of burnt flesh went all over my new coat. I never could wear it again. After that I didn't attend any more executions.

"And that executioner — I heard later that he was killed. They said he was taking the electric chair somewhere — to St. Mary Parish I think they said — and that he had a car accident and was killed."

The year 1949 brought personal sorrow to Cat Doucet. His father, Lucius Doucet, 76, died at the family home on North Main Street, Opelousas, December 17. His was the second death in Cat's immediate family; his older brother, Hosea, had died several years previously.

In mid-August of 1951 the Cat gingerly stuck a paw in the political pot to test the temperature — to feel out his chances in the forthcoming 1952 elections.

Daily World readers were startled at this headline:

"Simon Stelly Backs Doucet for Sheriff."

The newspaper story, used with former sheriff Stelly's picture, was:

"A letter supporting the candidacy of D. J. Doucet for sheriff of St. Landry Parish has been signed by Simon Stelly and was made public yesterday — the first public move toward the parish elections next January.

"Doucet, who was sheriff from 1936 to 1940, is presently state parole officer for 10 parishes west of the Atchafalaya. Stelly, local businessman and planter, was sheriff from 1940 to 1944.

"Doucet was not available for comment on the letter, which

gave him the support of a former political foe. He has not announced his candidacy."

Exactly one week after this announcement appeared, another headline strengthened the case for Cat:

"Three Mayors Back Doucet for Sheriff."

The three mayors who wanted the public to know they were on Cat's side were Elvie Lanclos of Port Barre; Clinton C. Artigue, Krotz Springs, and J. M. Jackson, Melville.

The Daily World noted that this was the second announcement in support of Doucet within a week, but Doucet himself had not yet formally announced his candidacy.

The three mayors said they were prompted to support Cat for sheriff "by the present condition which exists in that office and the manner in which it is presently operated. We urge our friends to assist us in obtaining a change . . . . "

On the state scene, Governor Earl Long and former lieutenant governor Bill Dodd were fighting and feuding, calling each other liars and scoundrels right and left. A hard-hitting editorial in the Daily World took both Uncle Earl and Dodd to task, not sparing the third party in the dickering, Lucille May Grace:

"No matter how fast the tale unravels now, we must all keep in mind that this is Louisiana politics and that we shouldn't take it serious after all. It's like a never-ending bedtime story which fails to grow monotonous, even though repeated a thousand and two times.

"The only pity — all sides are fighting it out with your money and mine and while any side can win, the only losers all the time are — us."

The qualifying showdown brought some more surprises. Cat was lined up with a lady politician; also with a member of a prominent St. Landry family which had opposed him in past races, and an old friend from Arnaudville. It was a small ticket — Cat for sheriff, the other three for the Louisiana House.

The story was given due prominence on the Daily World's front page:

"Political hats sailed lustily yesterday into the St. Landry Parish political arena and at the day's end there were two tickets in the field — the incumbents, and one incomplete ticket headed by former sheriff D. J. Doucet — and competition for the incumbent representatives. The Democratic primary is to be held Dec. 15."

Three of the incumbent officials were unopposed: Henry Lastrapes, clerk of court; Lennie Savoy, assessor; Dr. Gerald Bertinot, coroner. Other incumbents on the Guilbeau ticket were Representatives Edward Dubuisson, Howard Lafleur and Sidney Sylvester, and State Senator Edward M. Boagni (Lessley P. Gardiner had served two terms in the senate, resigned when he was elected district judge; a special election placed Boagni in the senate seat).

Senator Boagni was opposed by an independent candidate, Wilson Moosa of Eunice. Senator Oscar Guidry of Acadia Parish had no opposition.

The newspaper story continued:

"Qualifying with Doucet were three candidates for state representative, Mrs. Richard S. 'Cubby' Parrott of Eunice, Edward V. 'Dud' Pavy, Opelousas attorney, and Wilfred Kidder, Arnaudville businessman."

Cat had managed to scrape up a couple of candidates for minor offices to add to his ticket:

"Also on the Doucet ticket for re-election are Henry Segar of Lawtell, justice of the peace, and Adam Darbonne, Lawtell, constable, both of the 18th justice court. Doucet said further endorsements would follow.

"Doucet served as sheriff of St. Landry Parish for the 1936-1940 term. He is presently state parole officer for 10 south central Louisiana parishes, and he served for eight years as a game warden and an investigator for the department of conservation. All told, he said that he has had 20 years of active law enforcement experience. He owns farms and has real estate in Opelousas.

"The Doucet group's qualifications yesterday ended speculation as to whether there would be any organized opposition to the incumbents, most of whom qualified last Tuesday."

So the Cat was going to try it on his own this time. His former running mates were lined up with the opposition. Even his beloved "Old Man Austin" was a political foe.

After 20 years, the old sheriff chuckles about the situation.

"Me and Austin, we were friendly enemies. We had some land together. We had a tenant farmer out there, but I was the one ran the place.

"After they got the crop in that year, I ran into Austin at the courthouse. He wanted to know when he was going to get his share of the crop money. I told him, 'not 'til after the election, because if I give it to you now, you'll use it against me!'

"He laughed about that. He knew it was true."

The sound of footsteps on the civil rights' stairway was first heard in St. Landry in 1949, when Negro residents of the parish asked for equal educational facilities. In 1950, for the first time in the history of the parish, Negroes were summoned for jury service, both grand jury and petit jury. The jury commission was ordered by District Judge Lessley P. Gardiner to replenish the jury box with 300 names, without distinguishing between black or white.

In October of 1951, St. Landry Negro citizens tried to register, but found the door of the registrar's office locked. The leader of the group, Richard Millspaugh, then walked across the street to the Daily World office and inserted a legal notice, notifying the sheriff and registrar of voters of intention to return.

A few days later the following appeared in the Mugwump column of the newspaper:

"The Election? We wrote that heading because among the notes on our desk was a reminder to remind you about this time to be sure to register for the forthcoming Democratic primary. Government by the people can't exist unless we vote: democracy functions best with the widest expression at the ballot box: and so on. But after typing that heading it occurred to us: The door is locked."

(Black people did register, for the first time since Reconstruction, a year later, after Cat Doucet was elected sheriff. A suit had been filed, but it never came to trial; the trial was unnecessary, because the key had been turned and the door was open).

Among the nine candidates for governor that year was one Kermit A. Parker, the first Negro candidate for governor of Louisiana since Reconstruction Days.

The other gubernatorial candidates were Hale Boggs, Bill Dodd, Lucille May Grace, Robert Kennon, Dudley LeBlanc, Cliff Lyles, James McLemore and Carlos S. Spaht.

Since he couldn't succeed himself, Uncle Earl was supporting Carlos Spaht, whose name proved a stumbling block in Cajun country: the Cajuns called him "Spit."

Speculation ran rife as to whom Cat was going to support for governor. He had always been a Long man; would he go along with Uncle Earl and endorse "Mr. Spit?" But Cat wasn't ready to talk.

Late in October Maxile Savoy of Eunice was appointed to replace Cat as state parole officer, the state job he had held for three years. Cat issued a brief statement: "I hope Mr. Savoy will be kind to the unfortunate and help them rehabilitate themselves, which is the prime duty of the parole officer."

About a week later Cat made the Mugwump column in the Daily World:

"That candidate for sheriff whom we mentioned as getting his printing done in Baton Rouge is D. J. (Cat's the Man) Doucet, who reports naturally he had it done in the Baton Rouge shop of Howard Strother, since the latter donated it to him as campaign assistance. So we can't blame the Cat: somebody give us something worthwhile, we generally accept it, too."

Thus the public learned of another turn-Cat — Howard Strother, former editor and publisher of the Eunice New Era, who had fought Cat's faction bitterly in 1940.

About mid-December political advertisements began to appear in parish newspapers and on KSLO, the Opelousas radio station (at that time KSLO was the only radio station in the parish; KEUN in Eunice began operations in July of 1952. There were two parish newspapers: the Opelousas Daily World and the Eunice News, which had consolidated the old New Era and the Opelousas semi-weekly, the Herald and Clarion).

The Guilbeau ticket bought a full page Christmas greeting ad in the Daily World, complete with pictures of the nine candidates on the ticket, including the unopposed candidates, Henry Lastrapes, Lennie Savoy and Dr. Bertinot.

After Christmas sheriff-candidate Doucet announced an addition to his ticket, Guy Gardiner of Acadia Parish, candidate for the Louisiana senate.

After the holidays the campaign swung into high gear. Cat's opposition bought another full page in the daily paper, probably designed to flush the Cat out into the new field of battle — the advertising media. It worked.

The opposition's ad was a Stelly boomerang. Someone had dug up an advertisement used by Sheriff Stelly in the 1944 campaign, which stated, among other things, that "Sheriff Stelly has abolished 'shakedowns,' 'kickbacks' and the sale of 'Saturday night permits' in the Parish of St. Landry."

Topping the re-published ad, in large bold type, was this challenge to former sheriff Stelly, who was now a Cat supporter:

"Simon Stelly, tell the people who you had reference to in the following ad which you published in the Daily World on Dec. 24, 1943. Didn't you succeed Cat Doucet in 1940? Who do you charge with 'shakedowns' and 'kickbacks?' What sheriff was short $25,716.70? You are on the stump and radio, tell the people the truth!"

So here was the 12-year-old skeleton in Cat's closet, dragged out in the open to remind all of the 1940 scandals in St. Landry, in which Cat had played the lead role . . . .

Three days after the ad appeared Cat's ticket bought itself a full page ad. The text of the ad, used with pictures of the main candidates, gave the platform of the ticket and a reproduction of a sample ballot. After that both sides held their big guns for the second primary.

The campaign had all the earmarks of an old-time, knock-down and drag-out fight. With one difference: all the charges and counter charges, the accusations of wrongdoing, monkey business and hanky-panky, were aired in paid political advertisements in the newspapers and paid time on radio. The days of free campaigning through news columns were over. Candidates were allowed to announce for free, with or without pictures, then print a brief digest of platforms. After that, except for what the newspapers deemed newsworthy, they said what they had to say in paid advertisements, or on the stump.

Four candidates tried for the sheriff's badge in 1952: Sheriff Guilbeau, Cat Doucet, Frederick M. "Mac" Allen and Leo B. Ford. But the real race, everybody said, was "between Cat and Clayton."

Returns of the Jan. 15 first primary showed Cat leading the field with 7.757 votes. Sheriff Guilbeau was right on his heels with 7,266. Cat carried 30 of the 47 precincts; a record 18,477 voters went to the polls.

Two of Cat's running mates won in the first primary: Dud Pavy for the legislature and Guy Gardiner (Acadia Parish) for the senate. The opposition also placed two of their men: Edward M. Boagni in the senate, and Ed Dubuisson, legislature.

The dust of the first primary hadn't yet settled when a large hue and cry about vote-buying blared forth. An editorial in the Daily World excoriated the practice, said to have been most flagrantly displayed. There were widespread reports of vote buying and selling in the parish; a mass meeting was called in Eunice by the mayor, Dr. J. J. Stagg. Vote buying must be stamped out, they said.

The crusade continued for several months. Judge Lessley Gardiner charged the grand jury to probe the matter; some 200 witnesses were heard, but the grand jury took no action. The judge declared he would charge the new grand jury with the same matter.

Meanwhile the campaign was revving up for the second primary.

Cat's opposition pulled another ace out of its collective sleeve. An anti-Cat advertisement published in the Eunice newspaper some 12 years before was dredged up and re-printed in the Daily World. The advertisement, under the heading "D. J. 'Cat' Doucet Under Federal Investigation" was a copy of a statement taken in the office of the Intelligence Unit at New Orleans on July 29, 1939, when some of Cat's former deputies were questioned concerning the kick-backs in the sheriff's office during his first term.

Two days later the Doucet-Parrott ticket came up with a page ad titled "D. J. (Cat) Doucet Answers: False and Libelous Political Advertisements."

It was stated in this rebuttal that "the testimony of certain disgruntled deputies . . . was not considered by the Department of Justice sufficient to warrant any action by the federal authorities and I was never at any time questioned, examined or interrogated in any way by any special agent of the Department of Justice, and to which I would at all times have willingly submitted."

Cat's apologia continued:

"True, during that extraordinary period following the defeat of Earl Long by Sam Jones in 1940 when many of our officials were charged with wrongdoing, some justly and some unjustly, charges were presented in the state court against me and likewise some of our parish and city officials growing out of unsupported charges of vouchers involving expenditure of public funds . . . only one of our parish officials was brought to trial. I was never afforded the benefit of a public trial and the pending charges against me were finally dropped and have now long since prescribed.

"I deny as defamatory and untrue published statements at the time and again revived for this election that I misued public money."

After Cat finished this defense of himself, he had a few nasty things to say about the opposition.

St. Landry residents not involved in the political melee found some humorous aspects in the reversed positions: Here was Cat fighting his old buddies, and the old buddies fighting back. Strangest of all, the Cat was lined up with his former enemies, the Pavys. No longer could newspaper readers identify the grandiose writings of Austin Fontenot in Cat's public statements. Instead, they speculated that the concise writing style of the printed statements was the work of another brilliant legal mind — Veazie Pavy — who had been, they suspected, the author of the anti-Cat propaganda used in the 1939 ad . . . .

On the state level, the 1952 primary election placed Judge Robert Kennon and Carlos Spaht, Uncle Earl's boy, in a run-off for governor.

About a week after the first primary, Judge Kennon found a stray Cat on his doorstep. The newspaper account was headlined: "Doucet Ticket Backs Kennon."

("I don't remember exactly how that was," Cat now says. "I guess it was part of the deal with the Pavys. It was them got me elected, you know.")

Asked for a comment on this new development, Kenneth Boagni, parish chairman for Kennon, told the newspaper that neither he or Judge Kennon had any comment, "except we welcome support of all groups."

The opposition, said Cat in a political ad, had actually come out for Spaht before the first primary; now they trying to cover up and pretend they were for Kennon, even though they were "doing all in their power to bring about the defeat of Judge Kennon."

Cat and "Cubby" Parrott made the most of their endorsement of the north Louisiana judge. They now called their ticket the "Kennon-Doucet-Parrott Ticket." Judge Kennon's picture was included in their political ads, also a sample ballot of the state election. Two Ward 1 police jury candidates also had the support of the Doucet ticket: Carroll J. Bertinot and Alvin F. Dohmann. The ticket solgan was "They're All Gonna Win!"

The Daily World devoted more than three columns to what candidates on both sides had to say at final rallies:

" . . . Doucet and Guilbeau face a run-off . . . closing what many have described as the most heated political campaign in St. Landry.

"Crowds of supporters for Doucet spilled over the courthouse at the Sunday night rally, packing the court room, its balcony, and crowding the corridors and lobby downstairs."

("I drew the biggest crowd anybody had ever seen at the courthouse," says Cat. "Not even Huey ever got a crowd like that!")

Veazie Pavy was master of ceremonies for the Doucet rally. Speakers, besides Cat and Cubby, included Senator-elect Guy Gardiner of Acadia; Representative-elect Dud Pavy; Alvin Dohmann, Wilfred Kidder, E. A. Veillon of Eunice; Bob Dejean and Simon Stelly.

"Answering what he said were charges made against him by the sheriff, Doucet shouted: 'I have property because I didn't drink whiskey and invest my money in the race horses!'"

Sheriff Guilbeau had a few things to say also. Answering Cat's claim that he, Cat, 'ran the sheriff's office when I was a deputy,' the sheriff said: "He at no time ran my office — he only ran it down!"

The official vote count after the run-off gave Cat a comfortable 726-vote lead over Sheriff Guilbeau. Some 19,500 persons balloted in the sheriff's race.

This was a smashing victory, a real "landscape," considering . . .

"Cubby" Parrott went in also, and became the first woman from St. Landry Parish to be elected to the House of Representatives. Cubby polled even more votes than Cat: 10,962 to Cat's 10,019.

Judge Robert Kennon, under whose flag Cat had elected to fight, won the governor's race over Carlos Spaht, the Long candidate.

The election had been quiet, the Daily World reported. The editor (and Mugwump column writer), who had started the anti-vote buying crusade, had some pertinent comments:

"Casual checks at various polling places, reports from others, and remarks by others here and there, indicate that yesterday's election was one of the quietest and best conducted in St. Landry Parish history, despite its having had one of the highest votes ever recorded.

"There was less crowding around the polling places.

"People went and voted, then went away.

"The vote hustlers and car drivers for the two factions carried on their business more discreetly. What vote buying there was (and the understanding is that there was some) was mighty discreet.

"There was less assistance given at most polls than was the case in the first primary. Reports from some rural precincts are that many more affidavits of illiteracy were made than had been done in the Jan. 15 voting. This may present investigators with some succulent information: If a voter made an illiteracy affidavit this time, and was on record as having voted on Jan. 15 but made no affidavit in that primary, some embarrassing questions can ensue.

93

"Speculation is that some of the 'bought' vote was done 'on faith.' Far more people fixed their own ballots than before, fearful of signing illiteracy affidavits when they are known literates. If these people received payment, it was done by hopeful buyers, paying with no sure check on delivery.

"The vote-buying investigation, then, plus the 'schools' for commissioners and the general awakening of interest in clean elections, paid dividends.

"The lessening of vote-buying probably resulted in a more clear expression of the will of the people, and that is good."

During the spring of 1952, before Cat took over the sheriff's office, there was a crackdown on vice in the parish. This wasn't anything new. Periodically, through the years, Opelousas newspapers told of the closing down of houses of prostitution and gambling places.

Like the editor said about Louisiana politics, this was " like a never-ending story, which fails to grow monotonous even though repeated a thousand and two times." It happened during the tenure of every law enforcement officer, parish or city.

(It happened to Cat Doucet more often than most "because I was sheriff the longest," he says).

This time the "closing up of the cat houses" went all the way.

The front page story in the Daily World of May 6, 1952 was:

"One of Opelousas' most noted houses of prostitution has been shut down.

"City Police Chief Roland Chachere reported today that the house operated by Margaret Conger, 236 West Church, has ceased operations 'after 40 years.'

The shutdown came, the paper stated, as part of Chief Chachere's concerted drive to put a blackout on gambling and prostitution in Opelousas.

"The order was effective yesterday morning. Card games and other gambling are also shut down.

"Chief Chachere said he ordered his police staff to make "'a thorough check' of the city last night to see if any gambling or prostitution was being practiced.

"He said he had received no reports of any violations from his officers this morning.

"The chief's crackdown on any vice existing in the city is in cooperation with a request from Army officials at Camp Polk.

"The Polk officials, in letters to law enforcement officers in the area, asked that gambling and prostitution be checked in the interest of Camp Polk soldiers visiting this section."

Between the second primary and the time Cat was sworn in a rumor got around that maybe he wasn't going to get to be sheriff after all. Rumor had it there was some hang-up with the bonding company because of the 1940 suit against Cat and his bonding company.

This was cleared up through the Mugwump column:

"Incoming sheriff Cat Doucet has already made his $20,000 bond as tax collector and $6,000 as sheriff, and is ready to take office when his commission is issued after the inauguration. Maryland Casualty Co. posted the bond . . . that incidentally, squelches a rumor you may have heard . . . . "

Which may have suggested to some that Mugwump (John R. Thistlethwaite, editor and publisher of the Daily World) had either let his mug or his wump down on Cat's side of the fence. Not so. Mugwump alternately slapped and petted the Cat during the 16 years which followed, depending on how he (Cat) behaved, and what he (Mugwump) thought about it.

The sheriff and the editor however were not bad friends. Cat Doucet doesn't bruise easily; he didn't then and he doesn't now. A more sensitive individual might have yowled loud and long at some of the stuff printed about him. But not the Cat. He kept his inscrutable cool after a slap, no doubt figuring that eventually he would come in for his share of the petting.

A couple of weeks after this Mugwump informed his readers:

"D. J. (Cat) Doucet still hasn't announced his plans for deputies, either criminal or taxcollecting. But he says if anybody has any jobs open, he will be glad to recommend lots of people. Jobseekers are besieging him . . . "

Cat had indeed promised too many jobs. One story still being kicked around tells how he got out of this ticklish situation. Every job-seeker was received cordially by the sheriff-elect, the story goes. After each was reassured that indeed there was a job for him, Cat would ask nonchalantly: "How many words can you type a minute?" or "You can take shorthand, of course!"

Since the majority of the job seekers were country fellows with no special skills, this cut the list down quite effectively.

Cat Doucet was sworn in as sheriff of St. Landry on May 23, 1952. He announced immediately that he had assigned Simon Stelly as chief investigator attached to the sheriff's office. Mr. Stelly held this position the rest of his life.

(Cat had fought Simon, and Simon had fought Cat. This was in 1936 and 1940. In 1952 they joined forces and defeated Clayton Guilbeau. According to the plans for Cat made by "Mister Austin" in 1944, it was supposed to work the other way)

Four days after the swearing-in, a group of prisoners "vigorously requested presence of reporters and publicity" of their statements. The statement was signed by two prisoners from nearby Church Point (Church Point proper is in Acadia Parish, but many St. Landry residents have Church Point mailing addresses), two from Opelousas, and a fellow named Oliver Johnson of Greenville, S. C., who acted as spokesman.

The five prisoners told the Daily World reporter that their treatment and food had improved "100 per cent" since the new sheriff went in.

"Reading from a piece of brown paper Johnson said 'we wish to thank all of the people for getting a new sheriff.'

Johnson said he had been in the parish jail for 90 days on a burglary charge. He said foul language heretofore directed at the prisoners was stopped since Doucet went into office. "There's no more slamming doors in our faces," he declared.

"Johnson said that before Doucet became sheriff the prisoners were served 'nothing but rice. They would put a piece of meat on our plate but it would be mostly bone.'

"He said for breakfast they would get black syrup, two pieces of bread and coffee.

"'And for the last two weeks before the old sheriff went out they gave us nothing but coffee and bread — no black syrup.'

"Johnson said 'we now are getting bacon and eggs for breakfast and meat twice a day. We used to only get meat once a day.'"

The publicity given the "prisoner's song" moved Cat to action. He asked the police jury to increase the allowance for feeding prisoners from 85 cents to $1 a day.

("Most of the prisoners were from St. Landry and had relatives who could vote!" scoffed a hard-core anti-Cat).

The police jury took no action. In September Cat again registered a request to up the jailhouse food budget. St. Landry prisoners ate $664.53 worth of food during July, he said, and the police jury paid only $542.30 of the total bill. In June, the sheriff's prisoner food bill had amounted to $597.12, "and the jury refunded us only $458.12."

Cat argued that most of the parishes in the state got $1 a day for feeding prisoners, and the federal government allotted a minimum of $1.05 and a maximum of $1.50.

"I'll take the difference out of the sheriff's fund before I let 'em go hungry," the sheriff declared.

(Cat claims that he abolished the "kangaroo court" in the parish jail. New prisoners, unable to provide cigarettes or other items wanted by old inmates, were "tried" in the kangaroo court. Found guilty, the prisoner was beaten and otherwise maltreated by his fellow prisoners.

A parish resident, Mrs. Charlie Woods of Port Barre, wife of a Negro school bus driver, contributed a story that bears out Cat's claim that he did away with this ancient practice:

"My brother was put in jail. He didn't have any money and they beat him up so bad he almost died. That was before Mister Cat was sheriff. After Mister Cat got in, they said there was no more of that.")

During that first summer in office Cat merited a small bouquet from the New Orleans States and a brickbat from the Daily World. The New Orleans newspaper reported editorially on a "villainous game violation" that had been uncovered by the St. Landry sheriff's office, when four men had scattered poison in Lake Swayze in St. Landry Parish, "loaded up two trucks with the dead fish and sped off to northern markets."

The Cat and St. Landry

The brickbat was pitched by Mugwump:

"We didn't realize until reading his statement supporting John W. Clark for congress what an erudite and learned guy is our new sheriff D. J. (Cat) Doucet.

"Item: 'My friends and I unqualifiedly and without equivocation . . . ' How you pronounce that last word, Cat?

"Item: 'Mr. Clark . . . is intimately familiar with and has a deep insight into the problems besetting our nation . . . ' That word 'besetting' is pretty good, sheriff. Hits the spot.

"Item: 'Mr. Clark is well equipped . . . and will . . . work prodigiously . . . ' How you say it in French, Cat?

"Yep, our respect for the book l'arning of Sheriff Cat had taken a considerable jump since we read his illustrious and illuminating statement."

("Ah ha!" exclaimed Mugwump readers. "So Mister Austin is back in the picture!")

The congressional race was to get Cat in more hot water.

The Daily World of July 10 told the story:

"A heated argument sparked by the forthcoming congressional primary drew a crossfire of words and blows between Sheriff D. J. Doucet and Frank J. Hardey of Lake Charles, congressional candidate from the 7th district Tuesday night in a local bar.

"The parties involved gave conflicting stories of just what happened at the Tampico bar on the Eunice highway."

Hardey told the newsman that the sheriff had swung at him first, that he ducked and came up with an uppercut to the left side of the sheriff's neck, which knocked the sheriff to the floor. Then, Hardey said, he "jumped on" the sheriff and "two bullies had to pull me off him."

One of the "bullies" hit him in the back, Hardey said, then the two of them took him outside and tried to beat him up.

Cat said it wasn't so. He said Hardey was drunk, that he did not swing at him, and that Hardey hadn't hit him: "he just scratched the side of my face." What's more, the sheriff averred, he had not been knocked down. He had tripped on a chair.

As it turned out, neither Hardey or Cat's candidate, John Clark, won the congressional seat. T. A. Thompson of Ville Platte was the victor and remained in office until his death in a highway accident in 1965.

Later on that year Cat got involved in national politics. A newspaper story was headlined: "Cat Doesn't Like Ike." Another told that he and L. Austin Fontenot Sr. were in Washington, presumably to plan local campaign strategy for the Democratic presidential candidate, Adlai Stevenson.

Some weeks later Sheriff Doucet and four attorneys went on the air via Opelousas radio for the Stevenson-Sparkman ticket. Speaking with Cat were L. Austin Fontenot Sr., Leon S. Haas Jr., and Morgan Goudeau III, all of Opelousas, and Al Tate Jr. of Ville Platte.

Cat didn't win that election either. A lot of other people "liked Ike."

No sooner had Cat taken office than citizens started screaming about "vice and prostitution." This hydra-headed monster was to be his *"bête noir"* for the next 16 years.

In mid-July of 1952, H. B. "Pete" Dejean, Opelousas city marshal, staged a clean-up drive that he said wiped out "flagrant instances of prostitution" being conducted in three establshments just west of Opelousas on the Eunice highway: Penny's Place, the Tampico Hotel and West End Club.

Marshal Dejean said he had been approached by a group of citizens who lived in the vicinity of the establishments, that he had made a personal investigation and found the charges "well founded." He made it clear that his jurisdiction was concurrent with that of the police chief and the sheriff.

Cat took the ball. He and his deputies, he said next day in a printed statement, had been making nightly inspection of places of business "from parish line to parish line" for a month, and had found no evidence of any prostitution going on in any of them.

"When we do find evidence you can be sure they'll be arrested and brought before Judge Gardiner," he said.

Maybe Pete had some evidence that wrongdoing was going on, said Cat, but his department had not. "I'm glad he took action. We all want to work together.

"I was at Tampico Saturday night," Cat added, "and absolutely

99

saw no evidence whatever of any prostitution." Sure, he said, those places have girls working, but "how can you stop girls from working?"

("Yeah?" said the unbelievers. "Sure Cat was at the Tampico Saturday night! He owns the property! The bartenders are his deputies . . . ")

Shortly before this incident the police jury had asked the sheriff to make "a proper investigation" of the operation of El Morocco Club, also west of Opelousas on the Eunice highway, and to turn over any law violations found to the district attorney. The jury had received a petition from residents of the neighborhood which complained of "noise" and "disrupted church services."

Cat did as the jury bid, reported back that El Morocco was "so quiet you could hear a pin drop" and promised his deputies would keep checking. He said he had arrested four women and three men even before the petition was circulated.

"The neighbors say everything is all right now," purred the Cat, and produced a letter from Father J. C. Gaudin, pastor of the new Our Lady of Mercy Catholic Church, which said "thank you sincerely, sheriff, for your prompt action."

Then came the marshal's clean-up campaign and on the heels of that, a suit filed by six residents of the area in question seeking a permanent injunction restraining West End Bar from operating "with prostitution on the premises" and calling the place "a public nuisance" infested with "pimps and disreputable characters."

In October of 1952 Negroes registered as qualified voters in St. Landry, the first since Civil War days. By January of 1953 Negro registration had become an accepted thing in St. Landry, and many crowded the registrar's office to place their names on the rolls.

Sheriff Doucet had appointed a long list of deputies, including five Negro deputies. Some of the appointees were honorary deputies, who served without pay, but were authorized to carry guns and preserve the peace in the parish. This had been a custom of long standing in St. Landry. Cards were issued to the honorary deputies, but none were sworn in.

The attorney general put a stop to that. He ruled that Cat couldn't do that anymore. The ruling made it mandatory that deputy sheriffs take the oath of office and furnish a $5,000 bond before discharging duties.

Thus ended a time-honored vote-getting device, which Cat had inherited from his predecessors.

The sheriff got favorable publicity in connection with a case that came up in December of 1952.

During the late afternoon of December 8 two strangers entered the Moonlight Inn, on West Landry Street in Opelousas. They had a few drinks, then demanded the money in the cash register. Jessie Manuel, the bar operator, thought it was some kind of a joke. But the strangers were not joking; one whipped out a gun and fired a bullet into the door jamb to show he meant business. Then the robbers forced Manuel, the bartender Evans Thibodeaux and a customer, Charles Greig, into a back room.

The bandits ordered the three men to lie down on the floor, then took their wallets. They then forced them, at gun point, to get into their car, drove to a wooded area near Krotz Springs some 20 miles away, tied up the victims with old rags and adhesive tape, and took off — with a haul of some $200.

An all-points bulletin was put out on the crooks, but no leads were forthcoming for some 42 hours. It was then that Edgar deLesseps, Daily World reporter, watching the teletype in the newspaper office, noticed a story about four men being held in Uvalde, Texas, after leaving a "125-mile trail of crime through south Texas." Several items in the wire story — the car model, the description of the German Luger gun — caused deLesseps to surmise these were the same men implicated in the Opelousas incident. He reported the story to Sheriff Doucet, who immediately began an investigation.

After checking with Uvalde authorities, the sheriff, with Manuel and Thibodeaux, took off for Texas to see if the two victims could identify the bandits. Two of the four men being held in Uvalde were indeed the "Moonlight bandits." After some negotiations with Texas authorities Cat brought them back to Opelousas to face charges of armed robbery and kidnapping.

The Cat and St. Landry

The pair, Benjamin C. Lofton, 31, of Miami, and Joe Eugene Richey, 21, of Terre Haute, Indiana, gave signed confessions to Sheriff Doucet. In short shift they were arraigned, pleaded guilty, and were sentenced by Judge Lessley Gardiner to serve terms in the state penitentiary. Lofton got 10 years and Richey three years. It was later learned that both were wanted in other Louisiana cities on similar charges. The crooks were carted off to Angola by Simon Stelly, chief investigator for the sheriff's office, and Calvin Folk of the Opelousas police force.

(Cat's son, Harold, contributed this anecdote which took place when Cat was driving Lofton and Richey from Uvalde to Opelousas to face charges:

Driving with the prisoners across the interminable Texas plains, the lawman's foot got heavy on the accelerator. Soon there was the whine of a police siren. Cat pulled off the road and the Texas state trooper came up to the car, prepared to write out a ticket. The sheriff identified himself and explained his mission.

"But sheriff," the trooper said. "You were driving 100 miles an hour!"

"You gotta drive fast to get out of this state!" Cat replied).

Early in 1953 Col. Francis Grevemberg, superintendent of Louisiana State Police, began his move to "close up the joints."

St. Landry residents nodded their heads and said "it's about time!" Charges of prostitution running rife in the parish were coming in from all sides. Eunice citizens were up in arms, and petitioned the sheriff to clean up "vice and prostitution" in the Eunice area.

Cat replied that he was "ready to meet with them, and to receive any evidence" they might have. The citizens came back with a request that the sheriff take "immediate action to bar such places of ill repute."

The sheriff defended himself by reminding that the matter complained of had been investigated by the grand jury the previous November, and that body had "failed to report any true bills." He stated that if anyone would make the necessary affidavit against any of the places in question, one of his deputies would make the

102

necessary arrests. He also reminded that there were officials in Eunice who would receive complaints: his Eunice deputy, Silton Jeansonne, and assistant district attorney J. Nilas Young.

The petition had been signed by heads of five Eunice civic clubs: Mrs. Claud Moody, Eunice Woman's Club; M. J. Fruge, Lion's Club; Jack Pucheu, Rotary Club; Eugene Picou, Kiwanis Club; Mrs. Joe Deville, Eunice Business and Professional Women's Club. The chief complaint concerned a bar and cafe one mile west of Eunice.

Then a New Orleans police officer charged that Opelousas was tied up with the largest prostitution syndicate in Louisiana. The charge brought denials from Sheriff Doucet, Police Chief J. G. Richard and Ward Marshal H. B. "Pete" Dejean.

Cat said he didn't believe there were "any such goings on" in the parish. But he announced he would go to New Orleans and look into the matter. On his return Cat reported that the city lawman told him the alleged prostitution syndicate was in operation "some time ago" and was "no longer going on."

Col. Grevemberg came to Opelousas on what he said was "routine business." But he told Opelousas reporters that the parish "would not escape" his hard-hitting raids. "When local officers don't fulfill their duty, we step in," the colonel added.

Cat took after people selling liquor to kids. Then Mugwump took after Cat.

The crackdown on selling liquor to minors came after complaints had been received by the sheriff and the district attorney. Cat warned all bars against sales of liquor to minors, and ordered deputies to keep a close watch on parish bars and to arrest all persons caught violating the law.

Mugwump decided Cat hadn't gone far enough. He pointed out that District Attorney J. Y. Fontenot had cited all laws concerning the sale of liquor, and had also said that prostitution and "B-girl" operations must stop. After commenting that Cat's attitude about minors being sold liquor was "laudable," Mugwump wanted to know "why the sheriff hadn't done anything about the Eunice petition for vice control, except ask for affidavits?"

A couple of months afterwards, in July, Col. Grevemberg and

his troopers sharpened their axes for all-out warfare on any form of gambling. A deadline was given to close down all places of gambling.

That's when the Cat defied the Colonel.

"I'm not arresting anybody who fails to comply with that order," Cat said. "These people have paid licenses to operate those machines, both federal and state license. It's not fair to make them take the machines out."

Justifying his stand, Cat added:

"You can't make a man pay for a license then close him up if he refuses to throw out the machines. It don't make sense."

The sheriff allowed that "they" could do one of two things: refund the license fee, or allow the businesses to finish out the year with the machines. "If there's any arresting to be done, the state police will have to do it," he said. He did, however, relay Grevemberg's order to the operators of businesses with automatic gambling devices.

The stand-off brought a measure of support for Cat from Mugwump:

"Sheriff Cat Doucet makes a telling point in his attitude regarding the current slot machine shutdown.

"Slot operators have just paid the state and federal governments sizable sums in licenses to operate the devices.

"The machines are illegal. Yet we, the people, through our legislators, have openly and legally slapped a tax on these illegal devices. To us, that action is a brazen example of public immorality.

"Slots being illegal, it is the duty of law enforcement officers, including the sheriff, to see that people are not allowed to operate them. But the lawmakers, in providing for a substantial tax on them, showed the expectation that the machines would be allowed to operate.

"In this situation, what does the law enforcement officer do? Does he enforce the law, which the legislators has shown it expects not to be enforced: If he does enforce it, shouldn't he have informed the owners of his intentions to do so before they laid it on the line to the state of Louisiana for the privilege of 'legally' operating 'illegal' devices?"

104

The Cajuns of south Louisiana didn't take too well to Col. Grevemberg's crackdown on vice and gambling. They had no objections to running off the bad women, and shrugged their shoulders at the smashing up of the slots.

But when the police superintendent bore down on church and American Legion bingo, raffles, poker and *bourrée* games, that was *"autre chose."*

Playing cards is a way of life for Acadians, both men and women. Long before poker and *bourrée* they played euchre, casino and a variety of other card games, some with rules they made up themselves.

And always for money. Or something, such as ducks, geese, guineas. Many an overcrowded barnyard was culled by card games. Never was there a Cajun who could see any sense in playing cards for fun. There had to be some stake in the game.

So when the colonel started that foolishness about bingo and card playing, it hit hard at the heart of *"la vie Acadienne."* Grevemberg got the back of the Cajun hand. They went underground.

The colonel and his troopers worked on the eradication of the "one-armed bandits" first. In September of 1953 the City Bar in Eunice was raided, two slot machines seized and the bar operator arrested. Capt. E. N. Gabarino of the Opelousas troop headquarters led the raid.

There were widespread reports of slot machines "hidden" around the parish in an attempt by operators to save the machines from the ax. Some weeks later troopers seized 33 slots stored in a camp on Bayou Courtableau, axed the machines, then had a bulldozer smash and bury them. Continuing the raids, they destroyed 46 slots found on a farm in the Gradney Island section of the parish. The biggest haul of "stored" slots was 68.

Gambling raids were made in Sunset and Arnaudville, also in the neighboring parish of Evangeline, at Ville Platte and Mamou.

An ultimatum was given the churches and veterans' organizations sponsoring benefit bingo games. Archbishop Rummel of New Orleans announced that Catholic churches in Louisiana would halt the practice.

The Cat and St. Landry

In the fall of 1954, during the church bazaar season, state troopers raided a bingo game at the Morrow Catholic Church and charged three residents of the area with conducting a gambling game. This was, the newspaper stated, the first "raid" on a church bingo game since state police had begun a rigid enforcement of the state's anti-gambling laws "more than a year ago."

Lt. Parker Fuselier of Troop K, Opelousas, told a reporter that he made the arrests after having received two complaints from a Protestant minister.

Lt. Fuselier and Trooper L. J. Veillon also raided a bar in Washington. They reported having gone through the back door of the bar-cafe and finding "two big poker games in full swing."

Red lights went out in St. Landry in October of 1954. Twenty persons were charged after state police raided three establishments, Margaret's Place on Church Street, Opelousas; Kilroy's Tavern, near Eunice, and Johnny's Place, Arnaudville.

On orders from Major Tom Burbank, Trooper L. G. Seale handed the charges to District Attorney J. Y. Fontenot. Arrested and charged with prostitution at Margaret's Place were six women; at Kilroy's, 12 women. These were the two best-known "cat houses" in the parish. The operator of the Arnaudville place was charged with selling liquor to minors.

St. Landry was not the only parish to wince under the "Grevemberg scourge." Simultaneous raids were made in 20 other places in 11 south Louisiana parishes.

In St. Landry the persons charged got out on $100 bond each and went right back to work.

Two nights later Margaret's and Kilroy's were raided again — "for the second time in a week," the paper reported. The names of the same persons charged in the earlier raid appeared again in the paper.

The big clean-up brought some problems for the state troopers also. Such as an incident that happened in December, 1954.

The paper reported that a Shuteston Negro woman was in the parish jail charged with prostitution, but the white "customer" who state police found in bed with her had been released.

"They could not find a legal charge to fit him," the paper said.

The woman's name was given, the "customer" identified only as a resident of Route 1, Church Point.

The story continued:

"A resident of the community complained to police headquarters that the residence was apparently used for prostitution, with cars arriving and departing at all hour and considerable disturbance.

"Lt. Parker Fuselier said that upon arriving at the locality he and Trooper L. B. Carriere were shown the house. Upon entering they found the man and the woman in bed together and arrested both."

Cat Doucet's second term in office was not marked with the spectacular criminal cases which had occurred during his first term (1936-1940). Only the usual run-of-the-mill crimes: shootings, stabbings, robberies, burglaries and such. And "vice and prostitution."

However, a new problem presented itself, one he had not dealt with before: labor disputes.

First there was picketing and minor violence at Opelousas Cotton Oil Mill, also a dispute at the Krotz Springs Gulf Refinery. Then came labor trouble at the Leonville Catholic Church, when a carpenter's strike halted work on the new $160,000 church building.

Word came that the picket line at the church was "wildcat" and manned by "goons from Lafayette." The union carpenters decided to return to work and ignore the pickets. Violence was feared.

Sheriff Cat took several of his deputies to the scene. They parked their three cars in front of the church and went inside to attend early morning Mass. While they were in the church two cars of Negro pickets, driven by two white men, appeared. They got out to establish the picket line, then eyed the sheriff's cars.

One of the leaders suggested they wait and talk to the sheriff. The other said "Hell no! Let's get out of here!" With that, they got in their cars and took off. That was the end of the labor trouble in Leonville.

This brought public praise for the sheriff from Irving Ward

Steinman of Alexandria, legal counsel for the General Louisiana Chapter of the Associated General Contractors of America, and from the pastor of the church, Father Alfred Gaudet.

Cat admits that this was the most peaceful settlement he had ever effected. All he did was go to church . . .

9

"As St. Landry Goes..."

Politics began to bubble up during the summer of 1955.

In August, Col. Francis Grevember, Louisiana's crusading state police head, whose name had been mentioned as a gubernatorial candidate, charged that gamblers Frank Costello and Carlos Marcello had put up $750,000 to smash his anti-vice campaign ... "Chep" Morrison, popular mayor of New Orleans, announced for governor in September ... four more hats sailed into the gubernatorial ring, tossed by Earl Long, James McLemore, Fred Preus and Grevemberg.

By mid-September, there were happenings on the parish scene. H. B. "Pete" Dejean, long-time Ward 1 marshal, came out for sheriff and announced his ticket: Dr. Fred Mayer for coroner; "Cubby" Parrott (Cat's lady running mate in the 1952 campaign), Sidney Sylvester (also a former Cat man) and Lee Mizzi, for state legislature; A. B. Smith and Gladney Manuel for police jury.

Next day Cat had his announcement in the paper, a full ticket: Henry Lastrapes, clerk of court, and Lennie Savoy, assessor (both now back on Cat's side); C. Kenneth Deshotel, John W. Clark and Wilfred Kidder for state legislature (Mr. Kidder later withdrew, for reasons of health, and Frank Diesi, a newcomer to the St. Landry political arena, replaced him on Cat's ticket). For state senate were Henry D. Larcade of St. Landry and Bill Cleveland of Acadia.

These were the candidates as announced by the two opposing factions. Other candidates qualified, mostly police juror and constable candidates not affiliated with either faction. Two independent candidates for major parish offices were Dr. Don deBlanc for coroner and Kenneth Boagni for senator.

Clerk of Court Lastrapes and Assessor Savoy ended up without opposition, a fine start for the Doucet ticket.

The campaign was unusually quiet. Voting machines were being used for the first time in a parish-wide election; candidates made a big thing of their "numbers." It was important that a candidate's number be remembered — voters who couldn't read could usually identify candidates by number. Numbers went with the names in political advertisements.

In order to familiarize the St. Landry electorate with the new method of balloting, several of the machines were brought into the parish courthouse before the election. Voters were invited to come in and "practice" on the machines.

Sheriff Cat, according to a "Cat tale" related by an Opelousas attorney, took full advantage of the situation. Any courthouse visitor who happened to be a Doucet supporter was personally escorted by the sheriff to the voting machine and given instructions on how to use it.

But Cat ran into difficulty with one voter. An aged colored man, one of the sheriff's loyal supporters, just couldn't understand the workings of the machine. Cat went over and over the procedure, still the old fellow shook his head in confusion.

Finally Cat gave up. He took out one of his political cards, which listed his name and number along with the names and voting machine numbers of his running mates.

"Listen, old man," he said. "You see that number on the top, number 57? That's me. When you go to vote, get in there and turn that little switch to 57, then get out of there!"

St. Landry Parish was long considered the "barometer" for state elections. Justifying an old adage that "as St. Landry goes, so goes the state," a Baton Rouge newsman, Ed Price, compiled figures on state elections going back 20 years. Only once in 20 years, said Price, had St. Landry's top choice for governor failed to be the state's first choice.

The saying held up for the 1956 election. Earl Long scored a smash win in the state and in the parish. Uncle Earl won in the first primary.

So did Cat. But his victory wasn't as smashing as Earl's. The Doucet majority over Pete Dejean was 1,216 by official vote count. Of the 23,586 votes cast in the sheriff's election Cat got 12,401 and Pete 11,185.

110

The Daily World wrapped it up:

"Sheriff Cat Doucet was swept back into another four-year term yesterday along with virtually all members of his ticket, as St. Landry Parish, the 'weathervane' of Louisiana politics, went down the line for tickets of former Governor Earl K. Long and his endorsee, the Doucet ticket.

"Once again the axiom, 'as St. Landry goes, so goes the state' was borne out.

"Most surprising feature of the parish race, in the face of the terrific Long wave in the parish, was the strong race ran by Doucet's opponent, H. B. "Pete" Dejean."

Besides the sheriff, the winners in the first primary were Bill Cleveland and Henry Larcade, senate; Kenneth Deshotel and Frank Diesi, legislature; Dr. deBlanc, coroner; Harry Frame and Buddy Fruge, police jury. Of these, all were on the Doucet ticket except Dr. deBlanc.

All had gone well on election day. Voting was slow, due to the unfamiliar machines, but no troublesome incidents took place. A couple of days later Mugwump had some humorous election "post mortems":

"Sheriff Doucet was smilingly greeting friends on the street with: 'They can't put the Cat out!'"

And:

"On the afternoon election day Deputy Simon Stelly unloaded large quantities of wine in cases at the courthouse, and had a colored man lug it into the sheriff's office. We thought it was in preparation for a victory celebration.

"But seems that Simon discovered that Walter Smith, a whole-hearted Pete Dejean supporter, had set up a private dispensary at the precinct near his farm, and was treating voters to a bottle of vino as a 'thank you' gesture.

"Grabbing his radio mike, Simon called the office and asked for a legal opinion as to whether a man could give away drinkables at a polling place on election day.

"They checked with the DA and radioed back that it was an illegal activity indeed (a person is prohibited from either selling or giving away drinking matter within a mile of any ward or precinct

111

in the state at which there is an election).

"So Simon confiscated the vino . . . but that Pete Dejean wine really flowed around the sheriff's office when jubilant supporters whooped it up as the returns showed victory . . . "

Shortly before the election a front page editorial in the Opelousas newspaper had proposed a change in the conduct of affairs of the sheriff's office. The lengthy editorial was titled: "Let's Plug the Crawfish Hole."

"It is 'way past time," the editorial began, "that St. Landry Parish taxpayers did something about the traditional conduct of the sheriff's office, and now, with the election to fill that office nigh, is a darned good time to do it.

"The situation to which we refer is not founded by the present incumbent and we are NOT aiming this at him, but at both him and his opponent on behalf of all the people . . . . "

The editor pointed out that the sheriff's salary fund was built from seven per cent of the state and parish tax collected by the sheriff. That the sheriff is authorized to spend the sum for salaries as he deems proper. Any money left in the fund is turned back for distribution to the school board, police jury, road districts and the like, in the percentage in which taxes are collected for each.

The trouble was, the editor opined, was that only one sheriff — Simon Stelly — had anything left in the salary fund to turn back. The money was always used up to pay deputies.

In the spring the paper carried the findings of the grand jury, which gave its report after a three-day session:

" . . . the jury apparently held no investigation into possible violations of the public payroll fraud law, which had been included by Judge Lessley Gardiner in his charge to the jury. The judge had promised both candidates for sheriff in the January primary that he would do this in an effort to end time-honored abuses of the sheriff's salary fund."

The editor wasn't about to drop his crusade. Each time the sheriff of a neighboring parish turned over surplus money from the salary fund to the police jury or other parish agencies, the story, under big, bold headlines, would be featured prominently in the Daily World . . .

112

Came the time when the audit report of the sheriff's department was published in a front page story. The money was all accounted for, in salaries to deputies and legitimate expenses.

The editor made one more attempt: to learn which deputies were getting how much for doing what. But he was stymied by lack of cooperation and polite evasion on the part of the deputies queried.

So, the editor announced in a Mugwump item, he "had quit crying in the wilderness."

That year was to witness the end, finally, of that most notorious of south Louisiana cat houses, Margaret's Place. The Daily World front paged the story on Feb. 29, 1956:

"An old-time Opelousas landmark went on the auction block today under orders from a federal bankruptcy referee.

"'Margaret's,' for 47 years a house of ill repute until padlocked by Francis Grevemberg, recently defeated reform candidate for Louisiana governor, was sold to Lloyd Andrus, local real estate dealer, for $4,700.

"Under terms of the bankruptcy sale, Andrus purchased the multi-roomed dwelling and a large lot from Anna Dupoyster (also known as Margaret Conger), long-time owner, as the highest bidder.

"Auctioneer for the distress sale was C. Kenneth Deshotel, Opelousas attorney and representative-elect.

"Plush household articles such as wall-to-wall carpeting, ornate mirrors and all the red light fixings were sold under the auctioneer's gavel, lock, stock and barrel, on a high-bid basis."

A sidelight story that was not in the paper concerned an out-of-state traveling salesman, a regular "customer" at Margaret's each time business brought him to Opelousas.

Shortly after the auction sale, the salesman came in on the train, got into a waiting taxi and directed the driver to take him "to Margaret's."

Whereupon the taxi driver informed him that Margaret's was closed down — for good — and the place sold at auction.

The disappointed salesman grabbed his sample cases, jumped

out the taxi and re-boarded the train, just as the conductor hollered "all aboard!"

The celebrated "madam" ended her days in an Opelousas nursing home. During her stay the nursing home staged a holiday party for the inmates, which was covered by the Opelousas newspaper. One of the publicity photos taken showed Margaret in the group around the Christmas tree, which caused Lillian Bourdier, long-time society editor, to quip: "At last Margaret got her picture on the society page!"

("Yeah," says Cat. "I knew Margaret. She was a good looking woman when she was young, and a smart woman too. She never gave us no trouble like at them other places. She didn't allow monkey business at her place. A fellow go in there and get drunk, she would take his money and his watch, things like that, and keep 'em for him 'til he sobered up.")

The Cat was mellowing; no doubt about it. Not once during his third term of office did he get into a fist fight . . . .

These were the years when racial barriers were being assaulted, and some were going down. Jazz, the music that came in after World War I, was being replaced by rock music which one psychiatrist termed, prophetically, "another sign of adolescent rebellion." The hydrogen bomb was being tested, the Russians sent up a satellite, "Sputnik," and the Ku Klux Klan tried a come-back in Louisiana.

Certain things Cat was still finding out the hard way. Like when J. B. Lancaster, state auditor, found that the sheriff had violated the payroll padding law by increasing the number of his deputies prior to the January election.

Cat said he was not aware that he was breaking the law; he had, he said, followed a practice long in existence in St. Landry in increasing the number of deputies in the fall of the year to meet a greater need for preservation of peace and order at dance halls and bars, whose business generally increased at that time of year.

The law prohibited an increase of more than five per cent in the number of employees six months before an election.

This brought a small echo of "the voice crying in the wilderness." Inserted in the newspaper account of Lancaster's findings was:

"Since the sheriff has followed the custom here of not filing his lists of deputies and employees and their salaries each fiscal year — as required by law — it is not possible presently to check the deputy-hiring policies of previous non-election years."

At the end of 1956 St. Landry registrations totaled 34,902. Of this number, 20 per cent signed the registration rolls with an "x". The proportion of white and colored voters was: white, 21,872; colored, 13,030.

Cat Doucet's re-election was rated the top news story of 1956, as had his election in 1952. The last issue of the Daily World that year announced that permanent voter registration would go into effect in St. Landry on Jan. 1, 1957.

The Cat got a "scat" from the grand jury at its 1957 spring session. The jury scored the sheriff's handling of prisoners, recommended that he immediately instruct his jailers and deputies not to allow anyone charged with a serious offense or a felony to be made a jail trusty.

What brought this on was the escape from the parish jail of one Jessie James Ferguson, charged with aggravated rape. Ferguson, a trusty, had "walked out" the courthouse the same day he was indicted by the grand jury, and at that time was still at large.

The parish jail continued to be a source of news for some time. A prisoner went on a hunger strike; the sheriff discovered five hacksaw blades and a ball of twine in the jail. Some weeks later a whole mess of jail-breaking equipment was uncovered: 21 hacksaw blades, six files, other items.

The year 1957 brought Audrey, first spotted brewing in Mexico's Campeche Bay on June 8. It took the vicious hurricane until June 27 to churn up enough fury to devastate the Louisiana coast at Cameron . . . 1957 was also the year when postage on first class letters went up from three to four cents . . . .

Mugwump took note of a bit of Doucet humor:
"Sheriff Doucet called early yesterday to report on that car that smashed into a store across the street from his house:

The Cat and St. Landry

"'He parked it right in the store,' the sheriff said."

Came 1958, and New Orleans Times-Picayune reporters claimed they found slot machines in St. Landry. Which brought some terse comments from the Daily World editor:

"That august 'Gray Lady" of New Orleans journalism, the Times-Picayune, 'took out' after State Rep. Frank Diesi, owner of Diesi's Restaurant, Krotz Springs.

"The Picayune, as is its custom whenever its ever-alert watch-dogs of the public morals find anything illegal in parishes other than Orleans — they never seem to find such illegal goings-on in the Crescent City . . . . "

In short, the editor said the "Gray Lady's" reporters had found a couple of slots in the Krotz Springs restaurant owned by Rep. Diesi and had made a federal case out of it in the New Orleans paper. The Opelousas editor, not condoning the outlawed slots, pointed out that the big exposé was specifically aimed at the state administration, and the editor saw no reason why his parish in particular should be the pawn in the continuing battle of the Longs versus "the lying newspapers."

At that time a reform movement in the state was pressuring Governor Long to do something about public gambling. Finally the governor ordered state police to "clean up the state."

This got the Cat's back up. Earl had promised "home rule;" this had been one of the major platform planks in his campaign for governor. The St. Landry sheriff said he could handle affairs in his parish without intervention by state police, and he wanted the governor to know it.

So Cat went to the New Orleans meeting of the Louisiana Sheriffs' Association to offer a resolution. The UPI, covering the sheriffs' meeting, sent this story back to the Opelousas paper:

"Sheriff D. J. Doucet's plan to castigate Gov. Earl Long for his use of state troopers in gambling raids was thwarted Thursday.

"The St. Landry sheriff planned to offer a reprimanding resolution at a meeting of the legislative committee of the Louisiana Sheriffs' Association here in New Orleans. But committee chairman Chester L. Wooten, of Plaquemine Parish, ruled that only legislative matters could be considered.

"The Doucet resolution urged that the governor and state police abide by the 'home rule' plank in Long's 1956 campaign. The plank maintained that local authorities should handle local disturbances, and state assistance used only if asked for by local authorities."

Cat's plan was "thwarted" but he got his message across just the same. The wire story was used in all the state papers . . . .

Gambling cropped up again some months later. A Times-Picayune reporter summarized gambling activities in the state, which led to questions on the local scene. But Cat beat 'em to the draw.

"All professional gambling in St. Landry is ended," the sheriff declared. The gamblers, he said, had "got out of control," and he had instructed his deputies to crack down.

As proof of his good work — to the world, to the press and especially to those invaders of his domain, the state police — Cat invited the Daily World editor over to the courthouse to see his "haul."

Sure enough, in two locked jail cells were stacks of slot machines, which Cat said he had seized at various places in the parish over a two-month period.

The sheriff asked Editor John Thistlethwaite and a bystander, Tony Chachere, to pose with him and the confiscated slots for a photo. The newspaper staff photographer, J. A. Bourdier, obliged with the pictorial evidence which was presented via front page.

The story said Mr. Chachere tried out one of the machines, hit three nickels, and put them in his pocket.

Editors being skeptical by nature, the paper checked with state police and got this answer: "We have had no orders to quell gambling."

Next day Cat gleefully reported he had a call from John Nick Brown, state police superintendent, asking that he clamp down on gambling. "I told him he was too late!" Cat bragged.

Then the sheriff invited the Times-Picayune to send reporters to check out his parish.

State police backed Cat's statement that professional gambling in the parish was closed down. Capt. E. N. Garbarino reported:

"the sheriff beat us to it."

This gave Cat a rest from slot machines headaches for almost a year . . . .

Political announcements popped like firecrackers right after New Years, 1959, and through the following months right up to qualifying deadline.

Joe Cropper, Opelousas barber, announced for sheriff early in January, two weeks later Percy Daigle said he was going to run (but he didn't).

Cat Doucet announced for re-election, with a full ticket, in March. In May, Adam Daigle, Eunice police chief, said he was in the running. Bill Dunbar announced for the sheriff's post in June, so did "Pete" Dejean. Louis Fontenot Jr. made his announcement in July. Maurice Cortez was also mentioned as a sheriff candidate, but his name did not appear on the list of candidates who qualified.

But six did run: Doucet, Fontenot, Daigle, Dunbar, Dejean and Cropper (And that's how they came out, in that order, in the first primary).

Cat's ticket, as announced on March 15, included his old standbys, Henry Lastrapes and Lennie Savoy, for re-election to their respective posts of clerk of court and assessor.

Cat also had Dr. Don deBlanc, now a courthouse "in," for coroner; Frank Diesi for the senate; Steve Dupuis, R. O. "Slim" Harris and Sidney Sylvester (back again on Cat's side) for state representatives. By the Sept. 15 qualifying date, however, Harris' name had been taken off and Ralph McGee's name added as candidate for the Louisiana House.

Louis Fontenot's running mates were Wilson Moosa of Eunice and Mayor J. M. Jackson of Melville for house of representatives; Dr. A. E. Williams, coroner.

Bill Dunbar's "People's Ticket" included Edward "Pete" Robin Jr., for assessor; Adam Daigle, sheriff; Dr. Fred J. Mayer, coroner; Dorris Godet, John Olivier and Newton Thibodeaux, representatives. Also: 13 police jury candidates, Rufus Carroll, Tony Graffagnino, Vernon Schwartzenburg, Gus Olivier, Willie Meche, Lennard J. Martin, James "Bubba" LeBlanc, Pete Antie, James Vidrine, L. T. Ortego, P. J. Gomer, Steve Lejeune, Harry Frame.

Pete Dejean had on his side Bill Barstow, L. V. Chachere and Easton Hebert for representatives; Harold Sylvester, clerk of court. And for police jury Vernon Schwartzenburg and Austin Wyble Jr. The Dejean ticket endorsed Pete Robin for assessor and Dr. Mayer for coroner.

A whopping 136 candidates for major parish offices qualified to run that year. The opposition was really ganging up on Cat, using the old "dual harness" device, drafting well known men from every section of the parish as candidates.

A lot of water flowed under Cat Doucet's political bridge in 1959. He had to defend himself against taunts of slot machines and segregation, right at election time. Plus answer charges that he failed to file his deputy list according to law.

His troubles were compounded by the onslaught of five opponents joined in a concerted effort to get him out of the courthouse.

Add to all this: the disintegration of a powerful friend and ally, Governor Earl Kemp Long. Then finally, at year's end, the loss by death of his best friend and counselor, L. Austin Fontenot Sr.

Cat's governor began to crack up in late May. The news hit the wires when his wife, Blanche, announced that her husband would go to bed at the Governor's Mansion, with physicians present, for several days. The 63-year-old governor had shown symptoms of severe mental strain in an outburst and blistering attack on his political enemies, especially the state newspapers.

Two days later the press announced that the "gravel-voiced governor" had been admitted to the psychiatric clinic at John Sealy Hospital in Galveston. "The last of the political red hot papas" had been brought to his condition by overwork and fatigue, Texas doctors said.

A date was set for a sanity hearing, in Texas, for the governor. And Cat Doucet was there.

He went to the Galveston hearing with L. Austin Fontenot Sr., John W. Clark of Eunice and D. J. Hode of Washington, La.

This is one story Cat remembers very well:

"When we got over there, Earl said: 'They hog-tied me and

119

brought me here in my shirttail. I had $9,000 in my pocket — they took it all, didn't leave me a nickel!'

"There were reporters and TV cameras everywhere. You could hardly move in that court room. Earl asked me: 'Boy, how much money you got?' I told him about $900. 'Well, give me $500,' he said. Austin give him some money too. He wrapped it in some newspaper. He told us, 'I'm gonna buy my way outa here!'

"He said, 'Cat, get your car and park it right in front of the courthouse. We're getting outa here!'

"I told him, 'we ain't gonna go far. They'll catch us on the ferry if not before.'"

The reporters and TV newsmen were edging up, trying to make out what the governor was saying to his friends from St. Landry. One TV newsmen cornered Cat, asked him who he was and why he had come.

"I told him I came to get my governor. I said, 'you already got a governor in Texas. You don't need two!'"

Cat got statewide exposure on that. The TV interview was televised from Baton Rouge.

Later, after Governor Long had gotten himself out of a Louisiana mental hospital by firing the hospital heads, he remembered the money he had borrowed from Cat in Galveston.

"He pulled out a bankroll," said Cat. "'How much I owe you, boy?' he asked me. He knew how much. He liked to argue. So I argued with him. But I got my $500. I needed it for my campaign."

When a Louisiana House committee began considering amendments to ease some voter qualification requirements, Cat went to Baton Rouge to air his views before the committee. He called for legislative action that would "let everybody vote."

"I'm in favor of letting people all over Louisiana vote," Cat said. "And I'm against putting them off the rolls because they can't read and write. Some people don't have an opportunity to go to school like Senator Rainach did."

(Senator Willie Rainach was a leading segregationist)

The committee chairman challenged Cat on the grounds that one of his deputies, one August Terrence, was a member of the NAACP.

Yeah, said the sheriff. That's true. This deputy is Dr. Terrence, a Negro physician, and like every doctor in the parish, he holds an honorary deputy's commission. Because, said Cat, "they have narcotics in their cars and make night calls."

Yeah, I have five colored deputies, the sheriff admitted.

The debate between the sheriff and the chairman grew heated; at one point a house sergeant-at-arms moved between the two. Just in time; Cat was getting his Cajun up and was ready to fight.

Like the time Cat went to the sheriffs' convention, the wire service reporters, recognizing good copy, made the most of his appearance before the committee.

Which cinched an even larger segment of the Negro vote for "Mister Cat."

Campaigning was brisk in 1959. There was a lull after the early announcements for office, but the action picked up in the summer.

Earl Long, free from the mental hospital at Mandeville, decided he wanted to run for governor again. He planned to succeed himself by resigning the governorship just before the qualifying deadline, at which time Lt. Governor Lether Frazer would take the reins and allow Earl to go a-campaigning.

Governor Long opened his campaign for re-election on July 4, speaking at rallies in Ville Platte and Eunice. The parish firecrackers really popped at the Eunice meeting; all of the six candidates for sheriff were there, and Sheriff Doucet popped the first cracker by charging that his five opponents were responsible for the "voter registration purge" in the parish.

A week later Cat started a "hand-shaking" campaign. He announced he would be in his office only until noon of each day, and would spend afternoons "meeting as many of my friends as possible."

Earl came to Opelousas the middle of August. The newspaper carried a front page picture of him shaking hands with Cat. The Long-Doucet rally drew about 500 persons, the paper said, "large for political rallies in St. Landry in recent years."

("Huh!" says Cat. "There was three times that many!")

From Opelousas, the Long people moved over to Church Point. Speakers included Oscar Guidry, candidate for lieutenant governor

121

on Earl's ticket, and C. J. "Bobby" Dugas, for state comptroller.

The reporter covering the Church Point meeting noted that the crowd of some 500 was unresponsive, and seemingly the people there had come more from curiosity than from interest. Crowds that heard him in north Louisiana were said to be "tepid" by state newspapers.

The governor's trial balloon never got off the ground. He ended up as a candidate for lieutenant governor on the Jimmy Noe ticket. He died of a heart attack less than a year later, on Sept. 5, 1960. Like Huey, Earl's head was "bloody but unbowed." A month before his death he had gotten himself elected to a seat in congress . . . .

Cat's "Old Man Austin" died on Nov. 7, 1959, in St. Landry Clinic. He was 80 years old. His obituary recorded that he was one of the most outstanding criminal lawyers in Louisiana, and recognized as one of the leading politicians of the state.

He had served two years in the Louisiana House of Representatives in the early 1900's; had been district attorney for St. Landry, a post now held by his son, J. Y. Fontenot. He had campaigned for Franklin Delano Roosevelt. His efforts had resulted in large scale flood control projects in Louisiana.

"Rarely did he lose a case," the obituary read. "He not only was a master of law but also had a courtroom manner that left its impact on jurors and spectators alike. His reputation as a criminal lawyer was known throughout the state."

He was a historian as well, and was particularly well versed in the history of World War II. He was buried at Cedar Hill Cemetery in Washington, and his friend, Cat Doucet, helped to carry him to his final resting place.

Cat had no time to sit around and brood over his loss. He had an election to win. He had five opponents; some of his former ticket mates were on the enemy side, there were reports of "slots whirling again." Cat said he "hadn't seen any."

Three of Cat's ticket mates were returned to office in the first primary of Dec. 5: Lastrapes, clerk of court; Savoy, assessor, and

Dr. deBlanc, coroner. Former representative Frank Diesi won his seat in the Louisiana Senate.

Cat lacked 1,316 votes of having a majority over his five opponents. He came out with an impressive 10,682 votes, but was thrown into a run-off with Louis Fontenot Jr., who had polled 3,358 votes.

As was expected, Daigle, Dejean and Dunbar threw their support to Fontenot. Together they had enough to make it hot for Cat in the second primary.

State-wise, Jimmie Davis and Chep Morrison were in the run-off for governor. Davis announced that he was backing the Fontenot ticket in St. Landry. Davis also won the support of Willie Rainach, one of the 10 other candidates for governor ousted in the first primary.

And that's how Cat became a Chep Morrison man.

The opposition's big guns let loose a barrage at Sheriff Cat just before Christmas of 1959, some two weeks prior to the run-off election.

Criminal charges were filed against the sheriff, citing his failure to file his list of deputies and the amounts of their salaries. The charges were filed by A. Veazie Pavy, Opelousas attorney and Cat's 1952 campaign manager, and Henry D. Larcade Jr., who had been elected to the state senate on Cat's ticket four years before.

District Attorney J. Y. Fontenot said he would look into the merits of the charge and "if I feel there is anything to it besides pure politics, I will then decide whether to accept charges."

The DA did look into the matter, then refused to accept the charge. The law, he said, applied to practically all public bodies— clerks of court, assessors, coroners, registrars of voters, levee boards. The law was, he said, "one of the most universally non-operative or unenforced laws in the state." Of the 64 Louisiana parishes, only seven sheriffs had ever filed such a report, and such had been on an irregular basis.

Within a few days of the election, the opposition made new demands to inspect the records in the sheriff's office. Editorially, the Daily World backed up the rights of citizens to examine the records, for whatever reason.

That's OK with me, said Cat. He said he would allow anyone, "Mr. Larcade, Mr. Pavy, or anyone else" to come into his office and examine the records. "I have nothing to hide," he said.

But, qualified the sheriff, they would have to wait until the tax rush was over. He couldn't have his deputy tax collector and clerks disturbed by a bunch of people wanting to look at the records.

"I'll have my deputy tax collector, Mr. Lee Dalfrey, make a list for Mr. Larcade, Mr. Pavy and the Daily World," said the sheriff. "But in 48 years no St. Landry sheriff has ever filed a list of deputies and their salaries with the clerk of court."

Pressed by the opposition, Cat put his foot down. He declared that the records in his office would not be available "until after the run-off." He tried to put his adversaries on the defensive: "They had eight years to do that," he said.

The adversaries came back with proof, shown in a Daily World ad, that they had made the request more than four months before, by registered mail.

The night before the election, at a Morrison-Doucet rally, Cat made public his list of deputies and their salaries. He released the list for newspaper publication the day after the election . . . .

More than 30,000 persons were qualified to vote in the run-off on Jan. 9; voting would take place at 52 precincts. There were 18 candidates for nine parish offices.

Cat kept his sheriff's badge by a majority of 2,237 votes. His total was 14,453, and Fontenot's, 12,226.

Cat's victory picture on front page showed him holding a poster inscribed: "Cat Did It Again!"

Fontenot was bitter over his defeat. On election night, after the returns were conclusive, he pounced on Cat and the voters in a radio speech.

The 1960 campaign was over — almost. Republican opposition in the sheriff's race, threatened four years earlier, finally materialized: John Dezauche qualified as the GOP candidate in the general election. For the first time since post Civil War days the victorious Democratic candidate for sheriff was not the sheriff-elect; he was the Democratic nominee.

Dezauche, a highly respected Opelousas businessman, posed no real threat to the Cat. The handful of Republicans in the parish rallied to the cause, but it took only two handfuls of Cat's Democratic supporters to smother the opposition.

The night of the general election, when Dezauche found himself overwhelmingly defeated, he telephoned Cat and congratulated him, complimenting Cat upon having run a clean and fair campaign, and offered assistance to his successful opponent.

Recalling Fontenot's bitterness, Dezauche's call prompted Cat to remark to his friends:

"That's the difference between ass and class."

This comment is now a "Cat classic;" it has been used time and again, revived and repeated, applied discriminately and indiscriminately.

"As Cat Doucet says, that's the difference between ass and class" is second only to "As Cat Doucet says, me, I talk out of my head."

Some "quotable quotes" originated during the 1960 campaign:

In a radio address, Clerk of Court Henry Lastrapes, wishing to acknowledge the new voting contingent, the black people, began his speech:

"Ladies and gentlemen and all you human beings . . . . "

Assessor Lennie Savoy: "My friends, our opponents say that Mr. Henry and I are too old to run for re-election. Let me ask you this: when you want to make a real good gumbo, what do you get? You don't go out and buy a young chicken — you get an old rooster!"

(After this, the two veteran campaigners were known around the courthouse as "the old roosters.")

During this campaign Cat handed out advertising cards printed on pink cardboard with his picture on, listing his name and number, etc. The opposition distributed identical pink cards, except the number printed after Cat's name was the voting number assigned to one of his opponents. The trick could have worked;

125

many illiterate voters balloted by number only.

During a radio address Cat heaped coals of fire on the head of an erstwhile supporter. He spoke directly to the man, addressing him by name, then slyly, quietly, turned the knife:

"We used to be good friends. Now I hear you're working for my opponents. You remember when we were real close? That time when your wife was so sick, and you were scared she would die and her people get the money she had hid in the old *armoire*? And you took that money and put it in the safe in my office? Then your wife got well and you put the money back in the *armoire* and she never did know about it!"

The old saying, "as St. Landry goes, so goes the state," went by the wayside that year. St. Landry gave Chep Morrison more than 5,000 votes over Jimmie Davis, but "the singing governor" went back for his second turn in the governor's chair.

Cat's candidates for the legislature, Sidney Sylvester, Steve Dupuis and Alton Durand, were the top men in the six-man race and got the three seats. Cat supporters went singing in the streets: "Hey diddle diddle, we got the Cat and the fiddle!"

A month after the election State Auditor J. B. Lancaster again complained about the increase in expenditures of the sheriff's department. Cat's list of deputies and their salaries, which he had also filed with the clerk of court as the law required, was all according to Hoyle, Lancaster said. But the record showed that 168 deputies got $132,524, an increase of almost $40,000 over the previous year. Only 24 deputies were full time; the rest were not covered by group insurance as required by law.

The sheriff explained. Those part-time deputies, he said, were deputized to keep order at night clubs and bars. "If I took out insurance on them part-time deputies, it would eat up the salary fund!"

The expenditures exceeded revenues by more than $20,000, Lancaster reported.

A misleading statement, said Cat, and was backed up by Deputy Tax Collector Dalfrey. They said the sheriff's office was not operating "in the red;" that on the contrary the fund showed a surplus of $87,229.43 at the end of December, 1959.

Cat said he had increased the salaries of regular deputies from $50 to $100 a month; the sheriff's department had bought two new cars. The salary increase, Cat said, was because of the increase in the cost of living and could be done "because we had a surplus of $64,710 at the end of June."

Auditor Lancaster did have one good thing to say. He ended his audit with: "the accounting records have continued to be maintained in an excellent manner."

10

"No Vice In St. Landry"

In late February of 1960 Mayor Chep Morrison announced to the press that the city of New Orleans would be visited in April by General Charles de Gaulle, president of the Republic of France.

The famous general, said Chep, was interested in meeting some of the French people of south Louisiana. "I know of no more fabulous French character than Sheriff D. J. 'Cat' Doucet," added Chep.

And that's how Cat got named to the welcoming committee for President de Gaulle.

Cat was one of the six from St. Landry and Evangeline Parishes invited to welcome de Gaulle. The six, Morgan Goudeau III and Sheriff Doucet of Opelousas, E. A. Veillon and Gladney Manuel of Eunice, Paul Tate and Calvin Landreneau of Mamou, made plans to drive to New Orleans together the morning of the reception.

But Cat decided to go down the day before (he doesn't remember for what reason), and as a consequence was among the people who welcomed the President of France when he arrived at the New Orleans airport.

"They made us stand in two lines," Cat said. "I was one of the first to shake hands with him. I said, *'bonjour, M'sieu le Presidente!'* We shook hands; he said to me, *'je suis fier d'attend la langue française.'* That means he was proud to hear me talk French to him."

A Life magazine photographer took a picture of Cat shaking hands with the towering general. The picture was used on the magazine cover.

Cat was in the motorcade that escorted de Gaulle from the airport to the hotel. At a private reception for the President and his wife, Cat spoke at length with the guests of honor.

"Mrs. de Gaulle — her name was Yvonne, same as my daughter's — she looked like Mrs. George Joubert of Lawtell.

I told her that. Chep Morrison could talk French too, not as good as me, but pretty good. I guess I was the one talked the most French to President de Gaulle. He could defend himself pretty good in French!"

President de Gaulle "talked French to the people for about an hour," Cat said. Next day, from a reviewing stand in front of St. Louis Cathedral, he addressed cheering thousands in English.

"Then they took him in the church for a ceremony. The priests threw holy water on him and all that. He wore his general's uniform and all his medals. And when the soldiers would pass in the parade he would salute every now and then. It was a great day."

The sheriff from St. Landry was impressed at the state banquet for de Gaulle. "That's the first time I seen that," he said. "They had something in a big bowl, like whiskey. They set fire to it and walked through the room with it burning. I remember that very well."

Cat's impression of the general:

"He was a very independent old gentleman. But sincere. Very sincere when he talked. He stood up straight, very dignified.

"I guess I'm the only sheriff that shook hands with three presidents. President de Gaulle and President Kennedy — he was senator then, and I met him at the airport and drove him in the 1956 Yambilee parade. And President Johnson, when he was campaigning for vice president. John Kennedy couldn't come to one of those $100-a-plate campaign dinners in New Orleans, so he sent Johnson."

(Morgan Goudeau III said he overheard Cat tell President de Gaulle: "I hear you been having some trouble with them Syrians. We got the Abbadallas and the Moosa in St. Landry, but they don't give me no trouble at all!")

On June 9, 1961, Jesse James Ferguson was executed at Angola for the January, 1959 murder of Joyce Marie Thibodeaux, 12.

This was the last execution to date (1972) in the state of Louisiana.

Ferguson was brought from the St. Landry Parish jail to Angola the afternoon before by Sheriff Cat Doucet and his son, Deputy

Harold Doucet. The Doucets, *père et fils*, were among the 15 persons who witnessed the execution.

The switch was pulled at 12:23 a.m. and Ferguson was pronounced dead at 12:32 a.m. Grady Carter was the executioner.

When the Doucets returned to Opelousas, Cat told the Daily World that Ferguson had spoken freely with his executioner; his last words had been to ask the people present to pray for him.

Ferguson's execution ended a court struggle of more than two years. He had been indicted by the St. Landry Parish Grand Jury in April, 1959 for the rape and murder of the young girl (both Ferguson and his victim were Negroes). The first trial, on the rape charge, ended in a mistrial.

Ferguson was convicted in June, 1959, on the murder charge, and was sentenced to death by Judge Lessley Gardiner. The Louisiana Supreme Court affirmed the conviction in March, 1960, and ruled against Ferguson's appeal in November of that year. His appeal for a hearing was denied by the United States Supreme Court.

The impending execution created no hubbub of sentiment, as might have been expected during a time of national racial polarization. Ferguson was an ex-convict; he had served time for crimes in Rapides Parish. He had also been indicted for the attempted rape of a Negro woman (he was the jail trusty who had walked out the courthouse the day he was indicted), but was acquitted.

The rape and brutal murder of the little girl (her body, left in an old warehouse, wasn't found for several days) was the type of crime that precluded sympathy for the condemned man. There was no talk of any attempts to secure commutation of sentence, as had been done in the case of Elgie Stephens in 1939.

The case of the state versus Jesse James Ferguson was quickly forgotten. Sheriff Doucet waited for members of the family to claim the body; no one came. After two weeks he gave Ferguson's body to Charity Hospital for medical research.

But Ferguson's name was to come up again in the years which followed.

In June of 1965 a United Press International writer did a story about death's row at Angola which pointed out that Jesse James

Ferguson of St. Landry Parish was the last person to be executed in the state. Other condemned persons who were in death's row at the time are still there.

It may be that Jesse James Ferguson of Opelousas, tried, convicted and executed during Sheriff Doucet's fourth term in office, will go down in history as the last man to be executed in Louisiana.

Slot machines kept Cat's name before the public in the spring and summer of 1962.

When the first complaints were registered, Cat said he "had enough of that."

"I won't allow slot machines," he said. "They ain't gonna make a monkey out of me and run me crazy for four more years about those machines. I'm gonna git rid of 'em all, soon as they come out."

Cat sent out his two-ton truck to make the rounds and pick up the slots.

"Every six-eight months we get an epidemic of them," he said. "I pick 'em up, then I put 'em in jail. They don't get 'em back."

But the district attorney ordered Cat to demolish the machines. Cat watched, sorrowfully, as 20 slots, which he had seized at rural stores and saloons, were smashed to bits under a scrap iron drop crusher.

"J. Y. told me I had to do it," he said. "I've been in the sheriff's department for 28 years and this is the first time I destroy other people's property."

The sheriff reported that he had a written order from the district attorney to destroy the machines, according to law. He said he had seized the slots after an article came out in the Times-Picayune.

He appealed to the "poor 'lil storekeepers to not listen to the operators and put the machines in." The operators, he said, had "gone around telling people it would be all right."

"This is no pleasure to me," the sheriff said as another slot went under the crusher.

The sum of $144.71 was found in the confiscated slots. The sheriff turned the money over to the parish Palsy Clinic.

131

The Cat and St. Landry

In April of 1962 Harold Doucet, the sheriff's eldest son, tried his hand at the political game. Harold, who had been a parish deputy, ran for Opelousas police chief against the incumbent, Roland Chachere, and won by a majority of 150 votes. The father-son law enforcement team came to be known as "The Cat and the Kitten."

About that time the Louisiana Sheriffs' Association decided it didn't want to fraternize with Sheriff Doucet of St. Landry. Acting through its president, Sheriff Bailey Grant of Ouachita Parish, the association returned Cat's membership card. The action came about on the basis of reports that Cat had supported two Negro candidates in the city election.

The wire service report said Cat denied such support, and quoted him as saying he thought Sheriff Grant "was misinformed by my political enemies."

A Daily World story said "the sheriff seemed perplexed" over the matter.

"The only thing I can figure out," said Cat, "is some sheriff from the Ku Klux Klan country is behind it."

Sheriff Grant had come to Opelousas two weeks before and returned his voucher for $504.16, said Cat.

"He was acting funny. Like a man who was on pills, or a man who had fell out of a tree on his head. He was nervous.

"I hardly know the fellow. Seen him two-three times in my life. I am 62 years old. I was in the sheriff's office when Bailey Grant was a boy running rabbits barefooted!"

Cat was eventually re-instated in the organization. But again the state spotlight had been on him. When the sheriffs' meeting took place Cat was surrounded by newsmen and TV cameras. Anything racial was getting to be big news.

Mugwump had some comments about the association's attempt at blackballing the Cat:

" . . . the sudden action by Sheriff Grant seems to reflect a sentiment about St. Landry which is prevalent among segregationist leaders from that part of the state."

Mugwump recalled that Rep. John Garrett of Haynesville had said St. Landry "is a powder keg" if officials did not mend their

132

ways, and "will explode into violent integration troubles" and the like.

"He charged officials here did not know what they are doing and that the situation is serious, indeed.

"We have this to say about Sheriff Doucet: We have heard him address colored gatherings on a number of occasions, and invariably he expresses the wisdom of segregation and urges maintenance of this way of life. And, perhaps oddly to people like Grant and Garrett, he gets a big hand when he says it."

Jim Garrison, New Orleans district attorney, took a swat at St. Landry when he made a speech in Baton Rouge in 1963. Garrison said there was "organized crime" in several Louisiana parishes, "including St. Landry."

Queried by the press about Garrison's charges, Cat answered:

"Some people have nose trouble. Last time Garrison opened his mouth it cost him a $1,000 fine. If he would attend to his own business instead of other people's business he'd get along better."

(Garrison had been fined on a charge of defaming eight judges of the Orleans Criminal District Court; his conviction was overturned by the United States Supreme Court in November, 1964).

"Garrison is misinformed about organized crime in St. Landry," Cat continued. "He can investigate crime in this parish after he is elected attorney general (Garrison had indicated he would be a candidate for that office in the December primary)."

The sheriff cited the last session of the grand jury to substantiate his statement that there was no organized crime in his parish.

Meanwhile "that deputy list" had come up again. Dallas Dupre, who had announced as a candidate for the sheriff's office almost a year before the first primary, filed the charge, but the district attorney said the charge "did not show violation." This was in the summer of 1962.

Four months before the election Dupre said he was prepared to file suit unless Cat filed a written itemized report showing expenditures of the sheriff's office.

Cat said: "Let him sue." The auditors, he said, were checking the books in his office; when the checking was complete, the report would be filed.

"But I don't have to tell Dallas Dupre when I am going to file the list," Cat said.

Couple of months later Dupre did file suit, which alleged that he wanted to show "wasteful and wanton squandering of public funds by a public official."

Cat's answer to that was: "One sure thing, Dupre's name is not on the payroll!"

Again the sheriff explained that the report was usually filed after the audit. The audit was now complete, he said, but his staff was busy collecting taxes.

"When we have time, the list will be filed. The records are open at all times for all to see."

Cat announced for re-election in June of 1963. He listed as running mates Lennie Savoy, for assessor; Steve Dupuis, Alton Durand and Sidney Sylvester, representatives; Dr. D. J. deBlanc, coroner, all for re-election.

"The grand old man of St. Landry Parish politics" was no longer in the running. Henry Lastrapes, clerk of court for more than half a century, had announced his forthcoming retirement.

In his stead the Doucet-Savoy ticket chose Lee Mizzi to run for clerk of court.

Some weeks later Austin J. Fontenot (no relation to "Old Man Austin") announced as an independent candidate for the Louisiana Senate, opposing Frank Diesi, incumbent. Senator Diesi had not been listed on the Doucet-Savoy ticket; Fontenot's announcement aroused considerable conjecture about a split-up between Cat and Senator Diesi. However, by mid-September, when the factions began to line up, Sheriff Doucet announced "despite rumors to the contrary" he was supporting Frank Diesi.

Cat had three opponents: Opelousas Mayor Percy Ledoux, Dallas Dupre and Joe Powers.

Rep. Alton Durand of Eunice announced he would run for the senate, later withdrew and didn't run for either office. This left Frank Diesi, George Joubert and Austin J. Fontenot.

Opposing the Doucet-Savoy legislative candidates Dupuis and Sylvester were Harry Garland, Gantt Nicholson, John Olivier, John

Esper Marionneaux, Newton Thibodeaux and Wilson Moosa.

Five candidates ran for clerk of court: Lee Mizzi, Howard Lafleur, Harold Sylvester, Herbert Castille, Clyde Doucet.

Coroner candidates were Dr. deBlanc, the incumbent; Dr. A. E. Williams, Dr. N. C. Lafleur (Dr. Lafleur later withdrew).

Assessor Savoy was the only incumbent with only one opponent.

There were 37 candidates, including two Negroes, for the 13 seats on the police jury (the original 11 seats had recently been increased by two). All of the 11 incumbents were up for re-election; seven were for Cat, two for Ledoux, two independent.

President John Kennedy died of an assassin's bullet in Dallas, Texas, Nov. 22, 1963, and St. Landry Parish suffered the trauma of shock and grief that afflicted the entire nation.

Sheriff Doucet felt a personal loss. This was the smiling young man he had driven in the 1956 Yambilee parade in Opelousas.

Cat's faction had scheduled a political rally for that night in a rural Negro community center. There was speculation that the rally might be cancelled because of the national crisis. No, said Cat, "we're gonna have it."

Meeting time, Cat was at the door handing out black arm bands to all comers. Later, making his speech, he commented:

"Looks like they're trying to kill all the good guys. First Huey Long, now President Kennedy. I guess they'll try and kill me next."

The Dec. 8 Democratic primary found Cat shy 253 votes for a majority over his three opponents. Voters gave Cat 11,282; Percy Ledoux, 7,882; Joe Powers, 3,107; Dallas Dupre, 799.

Two of the sheriff's ticket mates were returned to office: Assessor Savoy and Coroner deBlanc.

In the run-off for clerk of court were Howard Lafleur and Harold Sylvester; for state senate, Frank Diesi and Austin J. Fontenot; for two seats in the legislature, Steve Dupuis, Sidney Sylvester, Harry Garland and Newton Thibodeaux.

Again St. Landry "went for Chep." Morrison carried St. Landry by 8,248 votes; John J. McKeithen got 4,701.

135

The Cat and St. Landry

The Daily World gave the 33,701 parish voters (22,786 white, 10,915 black) something to talk about in the issue of Dec. 29:

"Diesi Formally Backed by Ledoux Faction" was the headline over the lead story.

Asked about his former ticket mate's endorsement by the opposition, Cat's answer was: "Give a man enough rope and let him hang himself."

After that both sides went hustling to get public endorsements. Harold Doucet, Opelousas police chief, and Wilfred Cortez, alderman-at-large, announced support of Austin Fontenot; the mayor of the Village of Cankton, Wilhelmina Savoy, the only lady mayor in the state, came out for Ledoux and Diesi.

In Eunice City Marshal Leonce Bellow, 16 city police officers and patrolmen, five deputy sheriffs and the town's dog catcher issued a statement endorsing Cat Doucet. The endorsement, they said, was "voluntary."

The Doucet-Savoy ticket had publicly announced support of Morrison before the first primary. The Ledoux ticket proclaimed its support for McKeithen.

A few days before the run-off the Daily World presented a report from the new political battlegrounds — the air waves:

"Sheriff D. J. Doucet lashed out at Sen. Frank Diesi, his former ticket mate in the first primary, in a short radio address here that was reminiscent of the personal political oratory of earlier days, and had much of St. Landry Parish buzzing with amusement — in some quarters — and dismay in others."

The sheriff, the paper said, was speaking on behalf of the candidacy of Austin J. Fontenot for senator.

"Doucet, a picturesque orator, took a few sideswipes at his opponent, Percy Ledoux, but he saved his heavy barrage for Sen. Diesi."

Cat jumped on Frank for voting for the "million dollar mansion" for Governor Jimmie Davis. "We needed that mansion about as much as a hog needs a saddle," he said.

Senator Diesi's restaurant at Krotz Springs had become a popular stopping-off place for travelers on north-south Louisiana high-

136

ways. Some 40 miles west of Baton Rouge and near the inter-
sections of Highways 190 and 71, the restaurant was also a convenient place for politicians to meet. The place came to be known
as "The Little Capitol" and Senator Diesi, proud of the appelation,
erected a tall sign bearing this title and a large reproduction of
the Louisiana capitol building.

Sometime after the Doucet-Diesi split-up, the senator received
a phone call from the sheriff.

"Hello, Frank," said Cat. "I know we're not on the same side
any more. But that's no reason we have to be enemies. I just
heard something I think you ought to know. There's a bunch of
Negroes going to have a sit-in at your restaurant tonight. I wanted
to prepare you."

The senator, realizing what a disastrous effect a sit-in could
have on his business, called together his Negro employees.

"If those people come in here tonight it could mean that I'd
have to close the restaurant, and then everybody here would be
out of a job. Tonight, when those people come, I want all of you
to go out and talk to them, and explain what can happen if they
come in here."

Accordingly, when two carloads of black people showed up
they were met by the Negro employees outside the restaurant.
They talked, quietly, for some time. Then the visitors re-entered
their cars and drove away.

The senator sighed with relief. He called in his black employees
to thank them.

"You handled that very well," he said. "Were you able to find
out why they decided to come to my place?"

"Yes, Mr. Frank," said the chief cook and spokesman for the
group. "I asked them. They said Mister Cat told 'em to come!"

The second primary returned Cat to the sheriff's office. He
brought most of his ticket mates with him. Voters gave Cat 14,039
and Ledoux 11,676, a majority of 2,363 for *"M'sieu le Chat."*

Austin J. Fontenot edged out Frank Diesi for the senate seat
(12,653 to 11,867); Dupuis and Sylvester went back as state
representatives, but Harold Sylvester beat Lee Mizzi (Doucet-

Savoy ticket) for clerk of court.

Another "job-seeker" story was circulated. Again this time, the story went, the demand for jobs exceeded the supply, like the Cat supporters who had been promised jobs as state troopers.

"You go on back home and get yourself a good haircut," Cat told each claimant. "Come back here Monday morning. And don't forget to bring your high school diploma. That big fellow out there at Trook K (Capt. Lonnie Rogers) won't hire nobody who don't have a high school diploma!"

The job-seekers had no high school diplomas, as Cat very well knew . . . .

An election always brought up "Cat stories." There is the one about the ward boss who approached Judge Lessley Gardiner when the judge, with Cat's support, was campaigning for re-election:

"Judge, I'd like to support you," the man said. "And I would do it if you'd get that low-down so-and-so of a Cat Doucet off your ticket!"

To which the judge responded:

"The day you can bring me more votes than Cat can, I'll take you up on that!"

The story got around to Cat. He went to the judge and said reproachfully:

"Lessley, would you do that to me?"

"Just as quick as you would do it to me!" replied the judge.

Judge Gardiner himself contributed this one:

"Cat was a notoriously soft-hearted sheriff, especially when the person in trouble with the law had a reputation as a good, law-abiding citizen under normal circumstances. Cat would come to me and plead for clemency for the fellow.

"'You know judge," he would say, 'this man is supporting his old mother. His wife left him for no good reason, and he's got some fine people in his family. Can't you go a little light on him?'

"This happened so many times that I knew what to say when I saw Cat headed for my office. 'Now look, Cat,' I would say.

138

'I know this man is a fine, upstanding gentleman, and he has six good brothers, seven virtuous sisters, at least a dozen honest uncles and goodness knows how many fine in-laws. And every one of them voted for you!'

"I thought I had his number. Then one day he came to plead the cause of a transient from Illinois . . . . "

The Cat, they said, would not risk antagonizing people in an election year.

Like the time an angry citizen came to his office to prefer charges against his neighbor for some reason or another. Cat listened sympathetically to the man's grievances, then said:

"That dirty, low-down fellow! Doing something like that to a nice person like you!"

Then he sent a deputy out to arrest the man charged. When the man was brought in, Cat frowned in surprise and asked: "What you doing here?" After hearing the man's side of the story, he exclaimed:

"You mean to tell me that dirty, low-down fellow charged a nice person like you with doing that?"

Edna Riseman Kurtz tells of Cat's politicking:

"I was so flattered when he came up to me, and in a confidential whisper said: 'I'm going to make you my campaign manager in your part of town!'

"When I got home my mother greeted me with: 'Mr. Doucet just called me. He asked me to be his campaign manager in this neighborhood!"

"I had to tell mama the truth; that this proved that Cat told all his women supporters the same thing. Which didn't faze mamma one bit. She answered: 'I know. But doesn't it sound good!'"

The whole parish knew that Cat used jailhouse labor to work on his farm.

One day in court the judge asked the sheriff: "where's the defendant?" To which Cat answered: "Well, judge, I'll have to go get him. He's out digging ditches."

Court had to be adjourned until that afternoon when the

139

defendant was brought in by the sheriff. The judge gave the sheriff a sound scolding.

No one ever made an issue of this illegal activity. Some of the lawyers talked to Cat about it, but he always had the same answer, one that was hard to refute:

"Them boys want to go out there and work. Wouldn't you if you was cooped up in a jail all the time? Besides, that keeps 'em healthy. Saves the parish money in doctor bills and medicine."

State Auditor J. B. Lancaster came to Opelousas to check out the sheriff's office for the year ending June 30, 1964, and found a comfortable surplus in the sheriff's salary fund, the first reported under Doucet administration.

Not exactly a bonanza that would set the parish agencies in a frenzy to get their share, but still a surplus — the sum of $4,299.67.

Some wag allowed that the sheriff must have been taking a 'Cat nap' and didn't know the surplus existed, else he would have taken steps to spend it, like hiring a few more deputies.

Auditor Lancaster was also "pleased to report the accounting records kept in an excellent manner," and that he appreciated the courtesies extended his representatives during the examination.

Prisoners were still eating good; "although the police jury allowed $14,181.40 for feeding prisoners, the audit showed it cost $20,616.95," Lancaster reported.

Largest item was salaries for deputies, which totaled $149,401.50. Other expenses included office equipment and supplies, telephone and telegraph fees, uniforms and badges, advertisements and tax notices, bond premiums, insurance; the cost of maintaining a fleet of cars, a boat for rescue work, also travel expenses. For a grand total of $261,178.86. Sheriffing was big business in St. Landry.

No matter how quiet and law-abiding the parish might seem during off-election years, somebody was sure to dig up something about "vice and prostitution" during the last half of an election year. This happened with such regularity that Cat supporters accused the opposition of tipping off the big city dailies.

The record shows, however, that it was always "open season" on Cat. Questions about vice and prostitution were apt to pop up at any time during Cat's 20 years as sheriff.

Cat was good copy, and the urban dailies knew it. The New Orleans and Baton Rouge reporters were, as Cat phrases it, "always on my back." They'd come "snooping around my parish" looking for something to write about.

And they'd usually find it.

In September of 1965 (an off-election year) Baton Rouge reporters said they found both slot machines and prostitution at the Spillway Bar on the Krotz Springs-Lebeau highway.

Cat blamed state authorities for permitting the re-opening of the place. He charged that "Baton Rouge newspapers are trying to embarrass the governor."

The bar in question, he said, had been closed four times "and three times the state has picked up their licenses then given 'em back."

"They don't have a parish license. I have refused to issue them one. They are open only on state licenses because the governor said they could reopen and would behave.

"I don't know what goes on there, but I haven't seen any roadblocks to stop people and haul 'em in there. The place is out in the woods, five miles from nearest neighbors."

("Taking to the woods" was an old device for places of ill repute in St. Landry and Evangeline Parishes. When complaints were registered concerning a "cat house" on a highway, the operators would simply move out and re-establish the place in the nearest woods).

In the fall of 1967 the Baton Rouge Morning Advocate published a front page story about alleged vice in St. Landry. The headline read:

"No Vice in St. Landry: Cat Says So".

The story:

"St. Landry Parish Sheriff D. J. 'Cat' Doucet said Thursday his office has investigated the Turf Club as recently as Saturday, but had found no evidence of gambling.

The Cat and St. Landry

"The Turf was mentioned specifically in a Life magazine article as being a gambling casino. It is located near Evangeline Downs, just over the Lafayette - St. Landry Parish line in St. Landry.

"'As far as I know,' Doucet said, 'they've never had any gambling there. I'm sure they have small games in the parish when a couple of farmers get together on Saturday night,' he added. 'But as far as big-time, organized gambling is concerned, I don't know of any in this parish.'

"Asked about a specific house of prostitution in the parish, Doucet said:

"'There might be two-three women out there, but I don't know anything about it.

"'In the first place, it's not an open proposition — you have to be known to get in — and besides, I keep away from that type of place,' Doucet said.

"'Since I don't go to those places,' he continued, 'if ever I'm put on the witness stand, I can honestly say I don't know what's going on.

"'If we get a complaint or something,' the sheriff said, 'we will investigate. But we have received no complaints about prostitution in the parish.'"

Naturally, the falcon-eyed Daily World editor picked up the Advocate story, added a few thoughts of his own:

"St. Landry Sheriff Cat Doucet, if he's one thing, he's consistent.

"Ask any Louisiana newsman.

"The sheriff has always had a ready answer for any reporter's question — particularly questions involving gambling, drinking and prostitution.

"Witness statements attributed to him this morning on the front page of the Baton Rouge Morning Advocate."

Cat was often misquoted, more often had his statements distorted. He never made a fuss about it. He had his own way of handling representatives from the news media.

Like the time a reporter from the Times-Picayune claimed to have found indisputable evidence of prostitution in the parish. The reporter telephoned the sheriff's office and asked Cat for a statement.

"I'll give you a statement," Cat told the man, "if you will print what I say exactly like I say it."

"Certainly, Sheriff," the reporter answered. "Just give me your statement. It will be printed verbatim."

"OK," said Cat. "Here's my statement, and you can say I said it: the way I look at it, a 'lil pussy on the side never hurt nobody."

The astonished reporter, speechless, hung up the phone . . . .

"Yeah, I remember that," Cat says. "I told him that. I wasn't feeling so good that day. Those fellows had been on my back for two-three weeks. He called me up and I told him that. He put in the paper that I had said something unprintable."

There is also the tale about the time when Cat's attention was called to the high cost of illicit love in the parish.

"That's a shame," he commented. "Those young fellows and them college boys, they don't have that kind of money. They ought to fix it like at the restaurants; you know, like a child's plate."

The retired sheriff himself volunteered a provocative sidelight on one of the "vice and prostitution" incidents that took place at some unspecified time during his tenure of office:

"They said I owned the property, but I never did own that. The senator owned it at one time. One day the governor called me up and said, 'Sheriff, we gotta close that place. Some tourists went in there. They thought it was a restaurant. They made a big fuss when they found out it was a cat house.'

"So I went out there and I told the man what the governor said. He said, 'Sheriff, maybe if I would move off the highway. You think the governor would let me operate if I would do that?' I told him I didn't know, but it would do no harm to ask.

"Me and the senator, we went to see the governor. I explained what the fellow wanted to do. The governor said, 'Sheriff, I have no objection to that. I guess them young fellows have to go some place.'

"The man moved the place off the highway, 'way back in the woods. You couldn't see it from the road — I had trouble finding

143

The Cat and St. Landry

it myself!

"Right after that the state police raided the place and closed it up again. Me and the senator, we went back to Baton Rouge to talk to the governor. We told him the fellow had done just what he said, moved off the highway where the tourists couldn't find him, but the troopers had come and raided him anyway.

"He told me, 'Sheriff, we just had to close that place again. A preacher from Shreveport went in there and got all drunk and went to bed with one of the women. Some of his friends saw him there, now his reputation is ruined.'

"I said, 'Governor, you tell that preacher he can go right there at Basile and buy himself a new reputation for $25!' He laughted about that."

He mused for a moment, rubbing his nose, a characteristic gesture. Then he added:

"It's all right for you to print that story, only it would be better if you wouldn't say it was a preacher."

He thought nothing of involving himself, the governor or the senator. His one concern was to protect the man of the cloth . . . .

11

"Goodby, Minou...."

Absentee voting was the big thing in the 1968 election campaign. On Nov. 18, 1967, absentee voting in St. Landry hit a new high, with 118 persons balloting in one day. Names of all absentee voters, as had been the custom, were published in the Daily World, on a day-by-day basis.

The number of absentee ballots continued to climb, despite an order restraining the clerk of court or his employees from giving assistance to absentee voters. One of the deputy clerks commented wryly: "Many people learned to read and write overnight!"

At the end of the absentee voting period four per cent of the registered electorate had cast paper ballots for a total of 1,511. Voter registration was the "largest in histry," said Ruby Moreau, parish registrar. Total registration was 37,431; 24,416 white, and 13,015 black

Cat had five opponents, among them a Negro school teacher, Charles Bryant. Others were Bill Soileau, long-time Doucet chief deputy; Jimmy Darby, Roland Chachere and a newcomer in the field, Adler Ledoux.

Ledoux was high man in the primary election with 9,771 votes. Cat was in second place with 8,459. The rest of the votes in the sheriff's race were divided thus: Soileau, 3,863; Bryant, 3,162; Chachere, 1,265; Darby, 295.

Returned to office in the first primary were Assessor Savoy and Clerk of Court Harold Sylvester. Dr. A. E. Williams was elected coroner.

In the Dec. 16 run-off were: Doucet and Ledoux, for sheriff; Diesi and Austin J. Fontenot for the senate; Armand Brinkhaus, Steve Dupuis, H. B. Dejean, Curtis Joubert, Sidney Sylvester and Wilson Moosa for three seats in the legislature (St. Landry had gained a third seat in a recent reapportionment).

The election campaign became more emotionally charged and personality laden as the run-off neared.

The Cat and St. Landry

The Ledoux faction coined a slogan: "Goodby Minou, Hello Ledoux!"("*Minou*" is a familiar word for "cat" among French-Acadians).

"Sizzling Election Race Nears Climax" said a Daily World headline. Observers said it was a "tight" race; only the flatly partisan supporters made any solid predictions as to whom would be the next sheriff.

Cat and Adler took part in a "first time ever" television debate.

The Daily World editor had some acerbic comments to offer about the sheriff candidates on television:

" . . . the candidates . . . swapped verbal thrusts for a lively half hour . . . they were talking simultaneously and energetically when time ran out . . .

"The program was billed as an interview by the station, a debate by the candidates, but came out a verbal wrangle . . .

"At the conclusion Interviewer Dud Lastrapes tried to secure 'last messages' but got, instead, an argument over who knew the law regarding the operation of ambulances by the sheriff's office . . .

(Cat told Adler: "You don't know as much about running the sheriff's office as I do about running a submarine!")

"It was typical St. Landry Parish politics — the art of government tellingly on display," concluded the editor.

Cat lost out to Ledoux by 968 votes in the run-off. Ledoux's total was 14,870 to Cat's 13,902. Seventy seven per cent of the registered voters cast ballots in the second primary.

Everything was over but the shouting.

There wasn't much shouting.

The general sentiment was sadness that "the old sheriff" would no longer be in the courthouse. He had spent 32 years there — 20 years as sheriff, 12 as deputy.

Cat Doucet was 68 years old when he was defeated. His children had grown up and married; he was a widower. Anna had died three years before, on Dec. 28, 1965, after a long illness. His "old mamma" had come to live with him (he cared for her until her death in 1970). His own health had begun to fail.

Just before the 1968 campaign he had eye surgery. His right eye had been damaged in a tear gas mishap while attempting to make an arrest ("they called me out there on the Grand Coteau prairie. A drunk Negro was beating his wife to death. I thought the fellow was in the house. After I used the tear gas gun I put it back in the car — it was cold, and I guess all the gas didn't come out at first. It came out and burned my eye. And the fellow wasn't even in the house! Next morning they had already made up. They came to my office together.").

A pinched nerve in the shoulder region had affected his right arm and hand; he had cataracts, a renal disorder, and "prostitate" trouble. The afflicted hand and arm had virtually disabled him; he couldn't see well enough to recognize his friends. During the campaign he wore a patch over the bad eye and had to be helped up to the platform or microphone.

"If Cat hadn't been sick," his friends say, "He would never have lost that election!"

Most of his foes agree.

"If he could get well and run again, he would win!" the friends contend.

All of his foes agree . . . .

What was the secret of Cat Doucet's durability as a politician?

"He was a diplomat; he always knew how to approach people," said Veazie Pavy. "He was hail and well met always; he made it his business to know people.

"Cat Doucet never stopped being a politician," said Judge Lessley Gardiner. "He was always a politician — 24 hours a day, 365 days a year. The man lived and breathed politics for every moment of his adult life."

"He never evaded an issue," said District Attorney J. Y. Fontenot. "He met everything head-on."

"Cat was unpolished and unlettered, but never uncouth," said Morgan Goudeau III, assistant district attorney.

Cat has his own ideas about how to survive in politics:

"Some of them boys in politics, they make mistakes. They

147

don't mix enough with the right kind of people. Them big shots —
they're gonna take off on election day, play golf or go fishing.
You can't make them express theirselves how they going to vote,
because they're afraid to lose some business.

"Them big shots, they'll put up the money for the campaign,
maybe a couple of hundred dollars, maybe 50 or 25. They think
they done their duty, see? Maybe they give to both sides — you
can't tell. Talking out of both sides of their mouth and whistling
'Dixie' in the middle!

"Them two-by-four poor boys, they get out and work for you,
talk on the street for you, wide open, you know what I mean?
They're not in business, they can help you and not hurt theirselves.

"That's the kind of people you got to mix with and show your
friendship. They the ones that's going to get out there and work
for you, kill theirselves getting people to the polls to vote for you."

Cat Doucet's contemporaries — those who knew him best during his years in office — agree on one point:

Cat was sincerely motivated in his efforts to help people,
especially the poor and the sick. They also agree that this facet of
his personality was responsible for his enduring popularity with
the rank and file.

Some of his beneficiaries offer testimony:

An aged Negro resident of Opelousas: "I always voted for the
old sheriff. Many years ago when my boy was in trouble, I needed
$65. Mister Cat got it for me."

An indigent white woman: "I was buying wood for the winter.
When Sheriff Doucet found out I was poor and sick, he told the
man not to charge me for the wood."

Mrs. Evelyn Norman, parish Welfare director (retired): "Cat
was forever after me to do something for the people he wanted to
help. When a case wasn't processed fast enough to suit him, he
would call me 'the redhead from the north.'" (Mrs. Norman came
to St. Landry from Avoyelles Parish, therefore "from the north.")

An Opelousas physician: "Cat sent people to my office every
week. The bills were sent to him. I don't know if he paid them

out of his own pocket or out of the sheriff's salary fund."

Hursey Richard, a former St. Landrian now living in New Orleans, gives strong evidence of the old sheriff's soft heart:

"We were living around Whiteville, in the country. My little boy, Vernon, got polio. It left him crippled. We took him to all the hospitals. When there was no more money I had to take him to Charity Hospital in New Orleans, leave him there, then go get him when it was time.

"I was so poor lots of times I didn't have the money for the bus ticket. I would borrow the money, just enough to buy the ticket and a few cents extra for Vernon to eat. I would sleep in the hospital waiting room and I could do without food 'til I got home.

"Once I was walking to Lebeau to catch the bus to New Orleans. Cat came along in the sheriff's car and made me get in. He wanted to know where I was going. I told him.

"He wouldn't let me get on that bus. He had one of his deputies take me to New Orleans to get Vernon. He told me never to put that little child on a bus again; to let him know about it, and he would see that we got there.

"This went on for 10 years. I never asked him. I don't ask charity of anybody. It was Cat that insisted. And that was, to me, more than money. It's something I can never forget as long as I live. I always supported Cat. And I got all my kin people to vote for him. My brother Wilfred wanted to vote for the other side. I argued with him. I said, 'vote for Cat just this one time, to help me pay back what he did for Vernon.' So he did."

There was also the matter of the black vote. Cat's enemies said that he capitalized on the Negro vote; that he saw the trend of the Civil Rights movement and made the Negroes believe he was responsible for getting them to vote. There were accusations of "Negro bloc vote" hurled at Cat during his three last campaigns.

"I'm the first sheriff that let the Negroes register to vote," Cat claims. It is a matter of record that they did register and vote for the first time in a hundred years when he was sheriff. And the record shows that black people voted in St. Landry much earlier

149

than in many other sections of the state, and that they did so without racial trouble.

Cat had real concern for black people, says Father John Barnett, S.S.J., long-time pastor of St. Ann's Catholic Church in the Mallet community:

"Some years ago I received a message that a boy of my parish had drowned. I went to the scene immediately. A man was in the bayou, above his knees in water and mud, searching for the body of the boy.

"I asked a bystander who the man was. 'That's Mister Cat,' I was told. Not a deputy or a subordinate, but the sheriff himself. After that, it didn't matter to me what they said about him. He had my vote."

The anti-Cats tell a story of rescue work in a Negro community after a flash flood hit St. Landry.

Several Negro children, wading through the overflow trying to reach high ground, stepped off into a ditch and were floundering around in the deeper water. Sheriff Doucet jumped into the ditch and hauled the children to safety.

"Couldn't you see those children were drowning?" he chided his deputies. "You should of been in there helping me save those future voters!"

Paul Mayne, Opelousas civil engineer, contributed this Cat anecdote:

"Back in the '20's, when Cat had a lively 'transfer' business driving customers to Margaret'c Place, Cliff Hebert operated an insurance agency. Cliff did his best to sell Cat some insurance on his taxi. But Cat's sales resistance held; he didn't say a definite no, he kept telling Cliff 'I'll think about it. I'll let you know when I'm ready.'

"Came the day when Cliff heard footsteps tearing up the stairway to his office. It was Cat.

"'How much that insurance cost?'" he asked Cliff. 'I'm ready to give you some business.'

"Cliff asked him to sit down and discuss the policy and the terms. Cat refused. Said he was in a hurry and wanted to close the deal. Cliff offered to make out the policy and mail it out, suggested Cat could pay for it at his convenience.

"'No, I want to finish with it right now,' Cat insisted. So Cliff made out the policy and accepted full payment.

"'That's all I got to do?' inquired Cat. Cliff assured him that all was in order, that his car was fully insured.

"'Well, that's fine," said Cat. 'Because my car just burned up on the Washington road.'"

Cat people and anti-Cats chuckle over this anecdote:

Once the sheriff was asked to serve as a judge at a beauty contset at a rural school in the parish. He accepted, thinking this to be a good opportunity to win friends and influence people.

However, when actually faced with making a final decision on the winner, it occurred to him that he could make more enemies than friends; the family and friends of the pretty girl he selected as winner would think he was a great guy. But what about the family and friends of the dozen or so losing beauties?

Quick thinking saved the day. Taking a cue from the applause meter used by Major Bowes in his talent show of old-time radio fame, Cat arranged all the girl contestants in a line on stage and announced:

"All these girls are so pretty I can't pick the winner. I'm gonna hold my hand over the head of each one. The one that have the most clap wins!"

One form of public exposure was explored to the fullest by Cat Doucet: parish funerals. The presence of the sheriff at last rites was as necessarily a part of the scene as the officiating minister.

Cat had his own little funeral ritual, says Didier Lafond, veteran mortician of Opelousas. Unlike some politicians who visit the funeral home, express sympathy to the family, sign the register and leave, Cat was always available when time came for the funeral cortege to leave the funeral home and proceed to the church.

This was when Cat walked out, usually just behind the priest and altar boys, but ahead of the pall bearers and people. It was his invariable custom to walk up to the hearse and open the doors

151

in readiness for the coffin.

During the years when Lafond and Son Funeral Home was located in downtown Opelousas the sheriff followed this routine. When the funeral home was moved out on the Opelousas-Sunset road, he changed his tactics to suit the situation. Here, the casket was moved out a side door as the mourners exited through the front entrance. The sheriff would park his car on the highway, pay his respects by being present at the brief religious ceremony which precedes the more solemn church services. Then, as the cortege slowly moved out en route to the church, every person attending the funeral had a good view of the traffic director, the sheriff himself.

Director Lafond also tells of the former sheriff's charity in hardship cases. Here also Cat had his own formula. He would call the funeral home director in advance and say something like this: "One of my friends lost a little child. They're gonna come with the body. You know what to do."

The director knew what to do — discount the bill and send it to Cat for payment.

(Cat didn't miss any of the funerals of state:
"I went to Huey Long's funeral, and Earl's too. And Dick Leche. And I was there when they buried Chep Morrison and Judge Porterie. But the one I remember most was when Judge Bob Jones died in Covington. I'll never forget that. When I got out of the car I split my pants from one end to the other, right down the back. I had to hold my hat behind me the whole time!")

Did Cat Doucet buy votes?
"Only when it was necessary!" sneer the foes.
"Of course," say the friends. "He bought votes for 20 years — with kindness!"

The "old sheriff" is not concerned with his place in history. Nor is he aware that his kind of politics no longer has a place in the changing scene.

Handicapped by illness, he sits in his armchair, his long legs crossed, and dreams of campaigns . . .

"If I would be elected again, I'd give half my salary to the Boy

Scouts and the Retired Children, things like that . . . "

His breathing is labored, his strong features flaccid from illness.

"I got a comfortable living from the farm and my rent houses. I don't need the money . . . "

The lower lid of his right eye, which has drooped painfully since the tear gas accident, is held up with adhesive tape.

"I couldn't see how to drive, but I wouldn't have to go out. I could have a deputy do that . . . "

His withered right hand is firm in greeting; his voice strong and without tremor; his smile, grotesquely crooked from the injured nerve, is confident.

"If I could run again, I would do it for them poor people . . . "

www.ingramcontent.com/pod-product-compliance
Lightning Source LLC
Chambersburg PA
CBHW070838100426
42813CB00003B/658